TH AWAKENING

Activate Your Pineal Gland & Develop Your Intuition

(A Guide to Repairing & Activating the Pineal Gland for Beginners)

Hattie Townson

Published by Kevin Dennis

Hattie Townson

Third Eye Awakening: Activate Your Pineal Gland & Develop Your Intuition (A Guide to Repairing & Activating the Pineal Gland for Beginners)

ISBN 978-1-989965-56-6

Legal & Disclaimer

The information contained in this book is not designed to replace or take the place of any form of medicine or professional medical advice. The information in this book has been provided for educational and entertainment purposes only.

The information contained in this book has been compiled from sources deemed reliable, and it is accurate to the best of the Author's knowledge; however, the Author cannot guarantee its accuracy and validity and cannot be held liable for any errors or omissions. Changes are periodically made to this book. You must consult your doctor or get professional medical advice before using any of the suggested remedies, techniques, or information in this book.

Table of Contents

Introduction

In the last couple of decades, various types of alternative therapies have been coming to light. Crystal healing is one such therapy, and it has become quite popular. Crystals have been used since the dawn of human civilization for their healing properties. It is believed that these stones help not just with healing, but they are also talismans of good luck, prosperity, and wealth. It is also believed that crystals can bring peace of mind to the wearer.

Since the 1980s, crystal healing has started to gain popularity quite steadily. A lot of people are using crystals these days from regular individuals to celebrities. It is being used as a means of healing and for luck. It is believed that crystals have certain inherent powers in them, and when this power is harnessed correctly, they can bring about certain positive changes.

In this book, you'll be given all the information that you need to start using crystals for relieving stress, anxiety, and trauma. By using different crystals mentioned in this book along with various techniques for using them, you can start healing your body, mind, and soul. You'll find information from the basics of crystal healing, to choosing crystals and using them effectively. This book will enable you to understand how you can re-energize crystals and use them to heal it is and improve your mental, physical, and spiritual health. If you never use crystals before and want to learn more about it, then this is the perfect book for you. Crystal healing is effective, and it is often used as a complementary and supportive therapy along with conventional treatments.

So, if you're ready to learn more about crystal healing, then let us get started without further ado.

Chapter 1: What, Exactly, Is The Third Eye?

How many eyes do you normally have? Well, you, obviously, know of two; the physical ones that are conspicuous and clearly located within your face. But there are, very likely, times that you see something for the first time, yet you have this feeling that it is not exactly new. Chances are that you had visualized whatever it is you are seeing now, but at a sub-conscious level. And much as we may be using sub-conscious here, in certain disciplines, it comes across as a level of, say – higher consciousness. At certain times too, you have this strong feeling about something and you may reckon it is your mind directing your line and density of thought, yet it happens to be a function of your third eye. So you cannot wonder that it is sometimes referred to as your mind's eye.

Has the third eye always existed?

From the old school of thought, the third eye has a lot to do with the mystical – some extraordinary ability to perceive things you cannot see with your naked eyes. In fact, in many cases, it is seen as ability to perceive things even before they happen; the reason the third eye is sometimes referred to as the speculative and invisible eye. Of course, since it is not visible it is also termed the inner eye. And, in a somewhat amusing way, in some faiths, it is even given a location. In Hinduism, for example, it is said to be on your brow – right between your eyebrows, but slightly above the eyebrow junction. You have possibly seen members of the Hindu community wear a red mark right on that spot.

In theosophy, which is a study of the divine within the Greek philosophy, the third eye is considered as being located within the pineal gland. This is a serious subject but it is sprinkled with funny aspects. When it comes to this discipline that is theosophy, for instance, it is believed that once upon a time – sounds like a tale of the ogres – the human third eye used to be physically located right at the back of your head (oops!). Sure – and it did perform both the physical role of watching and also the spiritual role of seeing the invisible.

Then, what the heck happened?

Well, ever heard that once upon a time you were monkeys? And then you learnt how to walk on twos and your brain developed somewhat and you became the bright beings that you are today? That is called evolving. And so, apparently, you may have had that physical third eye in those early stages of development, and it sort of dissolved or disappeared into your cranium (too much imagination here...), and now what you are left with is the ability to sense out-of-body things from your pineal gland.

Scientific perspective to the third eye

Incidentally, some highly educated people seem to see a lot of sense in the third eye and are trying to understand its mode of operation better. There is this doctor of psychiatry, Dr. Rick Strassman, who tends to see some link between the pineal gland and the excretion of the chemical, entheogen. Entheogen, for your information is said to induce different states of consciousness. So you see – the existence of the third eye is not a matter of mythical stories; religious hypnosis and fanaticism; or such other not-easy-to-believe practices. It is some reality that you may wish to appreciate; acknowledge, and even make use of.

And what is the modern sense of the third eye?

In the present day, the third eye does not change its basics since it is still invisible and not necessarily easy to comprehend; but it is associated more with enlightenment of sorts. It is also associated with your ability to understand and make best use of your chakras – those nerve centers that exist in different parts of your body, and which have a lot to do with your emotional, psychological and spiritual welfare.

In a religious sense, the third eye has got a lot to do with visions. In this respect, people who make good use of their third eye are often believed to be seers. On the overall, the third eye has plenty to do with non-physical experiences as well as precognition.

How, for the love of mystery and wit, do I begin to comprehend the third eye?

Yeah – if you are not into chakras and visions, you may be wondering what will make you understand the third eye better. Here is a case that will ring a bell:

Supposing your friend is grieving and you find that whatever words you prepare to say as a show of solidarity are not sufficient. Just being around this friend and showing empathy does wonders; your friend understands that you are communicating empathy and solidarity. You know what you are effectively doing in this case? You are utilizing the power of the third eye to send your heartfelt emotions to that person. The truth is that you and everyone else have the third eye. And evidently, your third eye does not just receive information, it also transmits it.

Another way of looking at the third eye

You know what a student portal is, don't you? The site where you log into and access whatever that appertains to you as a student – a place that is highly concentrated with information useful to you in particular and not the entire institution in general. That is precisely what your third eye is like – a portal that is concentrated with such great and positive energy, that it is able to sharpen your thinking and direct your focus. As such you find yourself with a high level of intuition; imagination; creativity; and also wisdom. And you can now see how you get to the high level of consciousness.

Does the third eye make you a psychic?

It is said that some people have their third eye open in a natural way, but you can also make a deliberate move to have your third eye open. Those people with their third eye very wide open from birth and they are aware of it are the ones you consider psychic. In their lot are some, in fact, who have been relied upon to help in criminal investigations because the energies of their third eye direct their focus on where the action is even without their physical presence.

Of course opening your third eye is not necessarily going to produce a psychic out of you, but you will, definitely, be more aware of your environment – the positive and negative energy within it – and even

9

be realistic about the possibilities of certain eventualities.

Chapter 2: Calcification Of The Pineal Gland

If you feel you are having trouble connecting with your inner spirit, you are certainly not alone. Unfortunately, most of the people on this planet are disconnected and living their lives without guidance from their inner selves. The result is living a life that is somewhat pointless, as there is no drive or desire, or even an idea of what we want. This is not a life worth living.

If you have any of the following afflictions, it may be that your pineal gland, the third eye as it were, is hindered. Take a look to see if you may identify with any of these things.

- Having a hard time making even the smallest decisions.
- No desire or passion for setting or reaching goals in life.
- Find no true joy or pleasure in your daily activities

- Trouble falling asleep
- Trouble staying asleep
- Fatigue upon waking and throughout the day
- **No sexual desire or sexual dysfunction**

You may notice that many of the symptoms here coincide with a diagnosis of depression, and that shouldn't be of any surprise. When the pineal gland is not making melatonin, and your sleep schedule is out of whack, the production of happy hormones, like serotonin, does not occur. The result is a tired, sluggish mind, incapable of anything but the bare minimum. If getting through the day is your only goal, you may have a blocked pineal gland. This isn't normal, so don't settle for good enough. This is your moment to find out what is wrong with your pineal gland, so that you may take action to live your best life.

Both the scientific and spiritual communities recognize the calcification of the pineal gland, or third eye, as a major cause of dysfunction in many aspects of life. The idea is that the gland becomes obstructed in some way that disrupts the flow of energy, and the production of hormones. Each recognizes the same culprits as the cause of this disruption.

Calcification is the process of mineral buildup. This can occur anywhere in the body as a result of too much of any mineral in the environment. This may manifest itself as kidney or gallstones, and this residue can build up around any tissue, including the pineal gland. These minerals disrupt the flow of energy and nutrients from the blood entering the gland. Think of it as a hard crust forming over the top of the gland.

Two of the biggest causes of pineal calcification are chlorine and fluoride. Chlorine is the chemical used to kill bacteria in pools and fluoride is added to water to prevent dental caries in the general population. While small amounts of these chemicals are actually necessary for the body in trace amounts, it is very easy to get overloaded with them.

The word calcification implies that calcium itself is a cause, and that is correct. Calcium is one of the most abundant minerals in our bodies, making up the structure of bone, creating muscle contraction and facilitating numerous reactions within the body. We need calcium, and many people are actually deficient. Taking a calcium supplement is very common, but if not taken correctly, could cause calcification of the pineal gland.

Calcium requires Vitamin D to be absorbed and utilized by the body. A lack of Vitamin D means that calcium will float around in the blood until it deposits somewhere. The result is calcification of important glands or deposits of calcium wreaking havoc in the kidneys.

Environmental toxins also play a big role in the calcification process. Any time the body comes in contact with a substance that is foreign to it, there is a question as to what happens to it. The body knows how to process food items and nutrients, but chemicals like pesticides and pollution are somewhat of a question mark. The body can certainly get rid of the bulk of it in urine or sweat, but some chemicals circulate in the blood and build up around the pineal gland.

High levels of mercury and lead end up in hair follicles and other strange places, and toxic levels can shut down organ systems altogether. The fact is, most of us are not exposed to large amounts of toxins like this, but the low-level exposures are still having a major impact on our wellbeing as related to the calcification of our pineal gland.

We must not forget about the things that purposely enter our bodies: food. The choices we make with food every day will affect the function of our pineal gland. When it comes to foreign substances, processed foods take the cake with their use. Preservatives and compounds not normally found in nature are now regularly added to foods to improve texture, quality and shelf life of food products. If consumed in large amounts, the excess has no choice but to settle in areas like the pineal gland.

The unfortunate reality is that our bodies are constantly bombarded with substances that can be harmful not only to the pineal gland but to our organ systems as well. Calcification of the pineal gland will cause a number of issues, starting with the decreased production of melatonin. This will quickly throw off your sleeping pattern causing general fatigue. The result of even a few nights of this can easily derail your motivation and quality of life. You may begin to forget things, be less productive throughout the day.

Over time, these small things add up to a major life issue. As your productivity slips so does that big promotion at work. You feel unmotivated to wake up in the morning, and even less so to explore the wonders of the world. With each day that passes like this, your inner self dims a little. Your brain and spirit become less and less connected, and your purpose and guidance completely disappear. You wander aimlessly, only focused on getting through the next few moments of your life.

True happiness is about looking at the big picture and leading a life full of wonder and purpose, all guided by your inner spirit. Knowing what you know now, how could you possibly go another moment with a calcified pineal gland. If your life could be exponentially better just by making some changes and decalcifying your pineal gland, why wouldn't you? Take some time to harness the information provided in the next chapter to begin the decalcification process.

Once your pineal gland is back up to speed, it will be possible to tap into its boundless potential and reconnect your brain and your spirit. Doing so will leave you with a bigger and a better sense of purpose, and you will live a life driven by infinite wisdom and ethereal guidance. Isn't that the life you want to live?

Chapter 3: Eye

Various systems of knowledge and teachings around the planet pay homage to a conceptual appendage known as the third eye. Also known as the inner eye or mind's eye, this aspect of the human psyche is responsible for humans'psychic awareness. Centrally located within the human brow, the third eye grants its owner the capacity to learn and act with a strong sense of intuition. It provides us with the answers that cannot be found in books.

The third eye is, like taste and hearing, a sense. While your physical senses such as sight and touch help you make sense of your physical surroundings, your third eye connects you to the metaphysical. Energy, emotions, purposes and higher powers are all perceived with the third eye. Your third eye has the potential to teach you everything that you need to know in order to work through life's greatest uncertainties. The concept of the third eye has groundings in several world religions, including Taoism, Hinduism, Christianity, and Buddhism. It also might have implications in neuroscience, particularly with regards to the human pineal gland, a grain-sized component of the brain.

Religious Implications

With a rich history of religious implications, the third eye is, unsurprisingly, highly regarded in cultures all over this planet. This section seeks to examine the religious contexts in which the third eye exists.

First, in addition to lesser known Chinese religions, Taoist teachings advocate for a practice known as third eye training. The Taoists wholly believe that the third eye not only exists but contains powers that, through meditative practices, can be cultivated and harnessed. A later chapter will detail the meditative techniques for awakening the third eye. Strongly associated with the sixth chakra, the third eye has a prominent place in Taoist traditions.

Second, Hindu cultures also hold the third eye in high regard. They teach that the mind's eye connects humans to realms of elevated consciousness. According to Hindu teachings, the third eye lies in the center of the human brow, just above the space between the uppermost points of the eye sockets.

Third, Christian systems of belief also refer to the concept of a third eye. According to prominent Christian leader father Richard Rohr, one who sees the world through their third eye possesses a holy mind and has the capacity to see beyond what two physical eyes permit.

Lastly, Buddhism and Buddhist teachings also provide evidence of the third eye's capabilities. To illustrate, many contemporary depictions of Buddha, including statues and illustrations, contain a dot or divot in the middle of his brow. This blemish symbolizes the third eye.

According to Buddhist tradition, the third eye gives seers the ability to perceive the world in extraordinary fashion. It is said to provide perspective, connect individuals to a higher state of consciousness, and bring about holy visions.

Pineal Gland Connections

In addition to its religious implications, the third eye has groundings in biological and psychological sciences. Namely, members of the scientific community believe that the pineal gland is the physical manifestation of the third eye. Because the pineal gland releases DMT during humans'first and last moments of life, it is said to be responsible for the holy experiences that occur during the processes of birth and death. DMT is a substance that naturally occurs in the human pineal gland. When extracted from plants and smoked by humans, it causes intense brief hallucinations that closely relate to spirituality and spiritual visions.

Consumers of extracted DMT report feeling at peace with themselves and in tune with their intuition after consuming. As such, the brain component that contains this entheogen is said to have ties to the concept of the third eye.

Along those same lines, the pineal gland is responsible for the secretion of serotonin, a mood-boosting hormone that readjusts people's attitudes towards the world. On top of that, it also secretes melatonin, the hormone that promotes the altered state of consciousness that we call sleep. The pineal gland, then, has the ability to alter the ways in which humans experience reality, both in waking and sleeping states.

Studies have found that when we interfere with the pineal gland's efforts to regulate sleep, when we stay up way after nightfall with the aid of artificial lighting, we increase our likelihood of developing horrid illnesses, including cancer. The pineal gland, by supplying melatonin, tries to make humans practice healthy sleep routines. However, technology, which indisputably advances more rapidly than evolution does, makes it so that we do not always listen to the messages that the pineal gland sends to our bodies. When you awaken it, you will find yourself more susceptible to the helpful, well-meaning suggestions that your pineal gland sends to you.

As a result of the increase in research conducted on the pineal gland, the connection between the concept of a third eye and the pineal gland often makes it difficult to distinguish between the scientific and spiritual implications of the third eye. Still, science is only one perspective in a holistic approach to considering the third eye. We must also take into account metaphysical, religious, spiritual, and philosophical perspectives as well.

Vestigial Theory

Some experts theorize that ancient humans possessed literal third eyes. In other words, people believe that the human face contained three nearly identical eyeballs. Over time, according to this theory, the third eye became vestigial. To elaborate, humans evolved out of the need for three eyeballs. As a result, the eye in the center became less and less prominent in each generation. Eventually, the third eye was no longer a visible part of the human face. Instead, it continued to sink deeper and deeper into the brow until it became fully internalized. The result of this evolutionary process came in the form of the pineal gland, the part of the brain that used to function as a literal, physical third eye.

So, if theories such as the above are to be believed, the contemporary third eye is a shell of its ancient form. Consequently, it lies dormant within the human psyche. As such, humans still have the capacity to harness the third eye's powers and capabilities; they only need to awaken it. In the following chapters, we will detail a variety of methods for getting in tune with the third eye and opening your psychic awareness.

Dangers of an Imbalanced Third Eye

The third eye has the potential to help humans achieve their spiritual goals and go through life with a sense of understanding, perspective, and purpose. However, a dormant or otherwise closed third eye can cause problems. The third eye regulates activity in the nose, pituitary gland, brain, pineal gland, eyes, ears, and neurological system. As such, imbalances and impurities within the third eye have the potential to cause a wealth of related conditions and physical dysfunctions, including headaches, depression, panic, nightmares, and eyestrain. Therefore, awakening and thus opening the third eye is essential for living a balanced, healthy life.

In addition, the third eye is responsible for intellect, application of knowledge, self-understanding, intuitive reasoning, visualization, and wisdom. Therefore, individuals with inactive third eyes tend to exhibit rigid thought processes that leave little room for possibilities outside of their respective perspectives. These unfortunate beings have little capacity to accept the possibility that truth might lie outside of their already firmly established systems of belief. In addition, they often have trouble leading their own lives, often relying on direction from sources of authority.

So, a person with a dormant third eye will experience a lack of empathy and direction. On the other hand, an overactive third eye can cause problems as well. Specifically, a person in possession of an overactive third eye will have difficulty distinguishing reality from fantasy. Certain methods described in this book will certainly push the boundaries of reality, but you do not want to be totally out of touch. As such, awakening the third eye in a healthy, balanced manner is key to the success of the methods listed in this book.

For example, hallucinogens, which will be discussed in detail in chapter 5, should be consumed in moderation, if you so choose to accept the risks and benefits that they can provide.

Chapter 4: Reasons To Activate Your Third Eye

Now that you are quite familiar with the fact that you actually posses "three" eyes rather than "two" eye and your third eye is as important (sometimes more important) as the two physical eyes, you would definitely be wondering why in the world should I activate my third eye when I am quite comfortable with the two.

Well, you are absolutely right about why should to bother to activate your third eye when you can see the world clearly through your two eyes. This is because you do not have any idea about what the third eye can do for you and what kind of different world you will be able to see through your third eye? Once you are able to experience the amazing things with this eye, I am confident you will want it opened for the rest of your life.

Although there are countless reasons to give this mysterious path of spiritual awakening a whirl, here are a few of the most important reasons to activate your third eye:

To Increase You Mental Abilities

It is noticed that most of us are unable to make quick and good decisions, this is because our mind is filled with so much confusion and fear that it takes forever to yield any result. If you want to increase your focus and improve the clarity of your mind, you will need to activate your third eye. Once you mind is clear from all the fear, ambiguities, and confusion and is focused you will be able to make better decisions and find simple answers to the very complicated questions very easily.

Manifest New Goals and Projects

We make decisions almost every day; these decisions greatly impact our future life. Whether it is about choosing a life partner or starting a new business project, if you are able to activate your third eye, you will be able to receive clear guidance and signals to make decisions that are most suitable for you. You will be able to witness ideas suddenly popping into your mind, you will enjoy many chance encounters and as soon as you start taking the first steps you will be surprised to see how quickly and easily things start to fall in to the right place.

To Discover a New You

There is another side of you that you have not encountered yet. It is only by deepening your connections with the spiritual world and peeking inside your soul that you will be able to find that New You. You will be surprised to find that there is much more to reality and consciousness than you previously thought. Once you are able to discover your New Identity you will be able to feel more powerful and confident and see yourself as a multi-dimensional being that is able to reside and travel in an interconnected divine world.

To Get Rid of Negative Energy/Thoughts

We are surrounded by negative thoughts/energy all the time, sometime these negative thoughts tend to overcome the positive energy and this is where the life starts to go downhill. Your third eye will help you to get rid of all the negativity from your life, this is because it will keep your mind, body and soul focused on only the positive aspects and ignore the negative ones.

Enjoy Better Relationships

Once you get rid of all the negative energy from your life, you will be able to see only the positive aspects in every walk of your life, whether it is a professional relationship or a personal relationship. With you third eye, you will be able to enjoy a much more rounded view of your life. You will be able to see and accept your own flaws and mistakes with open heart - the magical formula to enjoy better relationships.

All in all, we can easily say that your third eye will improve your day to day living and life in general. So do not wait another second and start practicing the methods described in this eBook to activate your third eye. In the next chapter I have shed some light on the some steps you can take to activate your third eye. Let us travel through this fascinating world together.

Chapter 5: What Is The Third Eye?

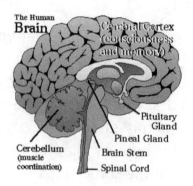

The Human **Brain**

Cerebral Cortex (consciousness and memory)

Pituitary Gland

Pineal Gland

Cerebellum (muscle coordination)

Brain Stem

Spinal Cord

Biologically speaking, the third eye is an adrenal gland known as the pineal gland. It is tucked deep inside the brain, between the right and left lobes. The gland is unique in that it is not isolated by a blood-brain barrier and is the last gland whose function was discovered.

The pineal gland is the size of a pea and can sometimes be seen in normal x-rays. The gland is known to calcify as a result of the body's repeated exposure to fluoride in water and toothpaste. Of course, this is more a modern day development as these products are relatively new in the scheme of society.

The gland's name stems from its appearance as it resembles a pine cone. The pineal gland produces a hormone called melatonin that controls seasonal moods as well as sleep patterns. It is said that the power of the third eye can be released by performing certain actions but all in all it is still not fully understood.

The location in the center of the brain has been of historically proportioned influence that can be traced back to the great pyramids of Egypt and beyond. Those in control of their intuitions were able to "see" at a different realm than others around them as is evident by the great monuments and other architecture left behind. Their ability to be in touch with the spiritual and physical worlds remains visible today.

Said to be activated by light, the pineal gland controls the biorhythms of the body. Hunger and thirst, basic needs, are also joined by the desire for sexual pleasure as well as the biological clock which controls the body's aging sequence. Known for its power of higher vision, the pineal gland has been known by some through the ages as the source of physic and supernatural powers.

The phrase "third eye" or "mind's eye" derives from the human body's ability to see something clearly in their mind...as if they were seeing it with their eyes. This is not to say that there is a certain spot the picture appears in a person's head as it is a complete mental experience.

The third eye contains the ability of astral sight. Astral images are seen through the third eye then transferred to the brain to process. Although the third eye cannot physically be seen as the other two eyes, it is very in tune with energy directed towards it. Auras and energy can be seen through the third eye.

Many scientists have studied the function of the pineal gland and many are doubtful that it really has the mystical abilities as some cultures believe. It has even been said that the gland releases a hallucinogen in instances like dreams or near death experiences. So far, these theories are yet to be scientifically proven.

The third eye is often located in illustrations and costumes placed just above the top of the nose in the center of the area between the eyes as a physical third eye. Buddha can be seen with a physical third eye. Museums are filled with examples, especially those of European derivation.

Chapter 6: Different Ways To Open Your Third Eye Chakra

Avoid Fluoride

Take serious considerations about the role of water in your life. Pipe water is a source of fluoride, which leads to pineal gland calcification. Fluoridated toothpaste is also a well-known source of fluoride in modern diet plans, as are inorganic and artificial drinks made out of contaminated water. Think about adding water filters to your sink along with shower faucets to avoid these high doses of fluoride that your body consumes every day just by taking a bath or washing your hands.

Dietary Supplement

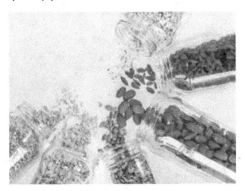

The list of dietary supplements that support and detoxify the third eye is long and includes raw cacao, garlic, lemons, goji berries, watermelon, honey, coconut oil, bananas, hemp seeds, seaweed, cilantro, chlorella, spirulina, raw apple cider vinegar, blue-green algae, zeolite, borax, ginseng, Vitamin D3, bentonite clay and chlorophyll. These are all elements that aid purification of the pineal gland.

Make Use of Essentials Oils

Many essential oils promote the development of the pineal gland, while facilitating states of spiritual awareness. These include lavender, sandalwood, frankincense, parsley and pine. Essential oils could be inhaled directly, rubbed on the entire body, burned on a diffuser, and also added to the bathwater.

Sun Gaze

The sun is an excellent source of power. Gazing softly at the sun during the first few minutes of sunrise and the last few minutes of sunset will do wonders when it comes to improving your pineal gland.

Use the Power of Crystals

Crystals are also influential allies in the quest for awakening the third eye. Utilize crystals and gemstones in the purple, indigo, and violet color palette. This color palette is a catalyzer to awaken, balance, align, and nurture the third eye. Try using amethyst, purple sapphire, purple violet tourmaline, rhodonite, and sodalite, as well. The procedure is simple: just place the crystal or gemstone between and slightly above the brow during relaxation, right where your third eye should be.

Let Your Feelings Shine

Once you start working with your third eye, you will start receiving guidance messages and also visions. Strive to have the courage to follow along with what your intuition offers, and, as you do this, your third eye strength will consistently grow over time.

Choose a Mantra

A mantra is a word or phrase you will repeat during your relaxation practice. You might choose to say the mantra out loud, or to verbalize it in your head solely, or even to enunciate it softly - that is a personal preference. Your mantra must be personalized and significant to you.

Your mantra must be something that you want to incorporate into your mind, or into your awareness. As an example, you might decide to repeat, "I select happiness." This can help support the idea that you are willing to focus on feeling pleasure all through the day.

Another useful mantra concept is to select just one word. As an example, you could replicate the word "Peacefulness." This will help spread a feeling of peace across your body and mind, which will foment the development of your third eye.

Be Mindful

Being mindful ensures that you are more positively aware of what's going on around you. You are intentionally paying attention to your feelings and natural sounds. Being more conscious will help you get in tune with yourself and the entire world around you.

As you are getting more observant, stay away from being judgmental. Just notice and also acknowledge without forming an opinion or a viewpoint about whether something happens to be "right" or maybe "wrong."

For instance, if you are experiencing stress, do not judge yourself for feeling that way. Simply notice and recognize your emotions. This is a crucial step in developing the full potential of the pineal gland.

Be Creative

Becoming mindful enables you to be more in touch with your creative side. Research shows that deep conscious breathing is an excellent treatment for writer's blocks, as well as for blocks that musicians and other creativity related professionals often experience. Being more mindful enables you to open your creative paths.

Consider experimenting with your creative side. Painting, writing, or learning a new musical instrument, are great ways of letting the juices of creation flow. Letting your creativity flow will assist you to feel much more in-tune with yourself, which will immensely help you to open up your third eye promptly.

Chapter 7: Third Eye Meditation Techniques

Visualizations help move energy to where you want it to go. This is because the mind itself is an energy receptor that can affect other kinds of energies. Visualizing is a form of meditation or controlling one's awareness to achieve a desired goal.

Meditation enables you to enter mental states that strengthen the third eye. Some meditative techniques are as follows:

- Visualizing a Cleaner and Stronger Third Eye Chakra

Picture your third eye chakra and pineal gland becoming healthier and more imbued with energy. Imagine healing and empowering light entering your forehead to cleanse the region of your third eye. See it glow in your mind. If you want to follow the chakra system, use indigo light since this is the color of the third eye chakra. As you do this, say to yourself that your third eye is increasing in strength and accuracy.

- Chanting or Humming

Since the pineal gland is piezoelectric, it can be activated by vibrations. Sit or stand with a straight back. Close your eyes and pay attention to the space where your third eye is. Inhale deeply, and upon exhaling, chant the mantra Om or any other resonant and meaningful word. You may also simply hum with your lips pressed together. Send the vibrations across your face until it reaches within your forehead. Keep your mind blank as you do this so that your thoughts won't interfere with the process.

- Receptive Awareness

Without thinking about anything else, focus your attention where you feel your third eye is. Allow images and ideas to form in your mind on their own. Do they tell you something about your third eye? You may receive insights about what to do to empower it. Remember them.

- Developing Your Chakras

Since the third eye is part of an energy system of chakras, you must take care of the other chakras to enhance it. There are many techniques for chakra development but the key is keeping yourself physical fit and releasing negative emotions, and thoughts. Visualize your chakras becoming clearer until energy passes freely through them. You may also seek the services of a healer or energy worker to clear your energy channels of blockages.

- Crystal Empowerment

Crystals are said to have their own energy and they resonate to particular chakras depending on their color. In general, indigo or deep blue crystals may be used for the third eye chakra. Some of the most commonly used for this are lapis lazuli, sodalite, sapphire, and amethyst.

Hold the crystal in one or both hands or gaze upon it while meditating. If you're lying down, place it on your forehead and imagine energy leaking from the gem into your third eye. When you're not meditating, carry it in your pocket.

- Practicing Affirmations

Affirmations are mental programs that aim to help the mind function in desired ways. These can help manifest reality via the law of attraction. There are many affirmations for psychic abilities such as the following:

- "I am ready to receive psychic guidance."
- "I open myself to the vibrations of the Universe."
- "I and the Universe are united."
- "My psychic abilities are becoming stronger and more reliable each day."

- "My awareness of the spiritual realms grows more and more."
- "My third eye chakra is becoming stronger every day

You can create your own affirmations but make sure they follow these guidelines:

- **Stated positively without not's or no's**
- **Simple and direct**
- **Expressed as if the desired goal is already attained or occurring**
- **Gives a positive feeling**
- Something believable

Recite these affirmations frequently while visualizing it happening in the present. Do this while in a receptive state of mind.

This chapter has dealt with techniques you can do yourself. The next one is all about getting help with third eye activation from other people.

Chapter 8: How To Begin To Open The Third Eye

Unfortunately, there are many substances in the average person's diet that will adversely affect the pineal gland or third eye. Having the correct diet will make it much easier to open the third eye, especially when you first try, once you have mastered using your third eye (and this takes time and best done under the guidance of a qualified teacher), it is reasonable to become less concerned with diet. One huge benefit from opening your third eye is that you will gain an understanding of the different foods that are best to avoid, as well as those that will complement and increase your abilities.

Almost all processed foods and animal products cause the pineal gland to calcify.

Many people who use their third eye will tell you their experiences have proved to them that eating meat, especially red meat, but also poultry and seafood desensitizes their empathy and their ability to use their third eye which is one reason not to eat meat. Another good reason is that meat produces an acidic condition in your body and this is not conducive to using the third eye. A vegan diet, especially a raw vegan diet is the best way to prepare your body and mind for opening your third eye.

Without a doubt, the most harmful substances you can eat or come into contact with is sodium fluoride. Sodium fluoride is in toothpaste and drinking water. The natural fluoride, calcium fluoride, which is naturally found in soil, fresh vegetables and other foods is a very different compound being natural and not toxic or harmful, especially if consumed in its natural state with the plants it comes with such as magnesium and especially calcium. These minerals counteract any adverse effects of fluoride, nature often pairs antidotes with poisons or designs complete foods that mitigate harmful substances in them.

The Sodium fluoride placed into water supplies and therefore also in most processed foods is a byproduct of many industrial processes, including producing aluminum and fertilizer, its main use is as a very effective insect and rodent killer, but it has very little use otherwise. Industry produces many millions of tons of sodium fluoride every year; some bright spark told a politician in the US many years ago that Fluoride was good for the teeth and that it would prevent tooth decay. At that time there was a huge problem with getting rid of all the sodium fluoride produce each year, it is so toxic that anywhere they dump it the land become a toxic wasteland. The solution was to put it into the water supply; they even made fluoride tablets that they gave to all school children. Sodium fluoride when ingested or even absorbed through the skin when washing goes straight to the pineal gland where it calcifies it and prevents it from working. (It is also harmful to the rest of the body and has no benefit to teeth at all).

During the 2nd world war the German, Russian and Japanese concentration camps used huge amounts of sodium fluoride in the drinking and washing water for the inmates to keep them docile and under control; they knew that it would block the function of the pineal gland and stop the inmates rebelling. This is a well-known fact. It is a matter of concern that even now that the US government is totally aware of the dangers of fluoridating the water supply, they still insist on making it mandatory for most states to keep adding it to the water. Why? Possibly they do not want people to start using their third eye. There is a lot of factual evidence to show that both the US and Russian governments have for years been developing third eye or pineal gland awareness within the military.

In order to be successful in opening your third eye or pineal gland it is necessary to avoid all the different substances that act to prevent it opening. It also helps to eat a good mixture of beneficial foods that contain the substances that nature has provided to assist you to open the third eye and increase your ability to experience it to the full.

The right or ideal diet for having a healthy third eye or pineal gland is a question that is hotly debated amongst those who are promoting or advocating opening the third eye. But it is generally agreed that a diet that promotes your body to be in an alkaline state is necessary and if your body is acidic it will inhibit the third eye. Generally, all alternative health professionals now say that the body is naturally alkaline and functions best when it is in this state. Unfortunately, most people because of their diet have a body that is acidic (this is also a reason why there is so much cancer and chronic disease).

The human body is designed to have a blood pH balance between 7.35 and 7.45; if you have too much acid in your blood it causes an imbalance that promotes diseases and calcification of the pineal gland. By eating acidic foods you force the body to try to correct this and neutralize itself, this it does by pulling nutrients out for other areas of the body causing further imbalances and making it difficult to use your third eye.

The pineal gland is not seperate from the rest of the body like the brain. This means that the pineal gland is not protected by the filtering system that protects the brain and attracts fluoride like a magnet.

People eating a plant based diet almost always have and maintain an alkaline body.

The standard diet consisting of such things as a breakfast of cereal, juice, toast margarine or jam, a lunch of sandwiches, pies, pasta, etc. and then a dinner of 2 to 3 vegetables (often canned, frozen or processed) and meat dish plus a sugar based dessert with junk food snacks, soda, tea/coffee and the 2 to 3 glasses of alcohol a day. Or those who have a diet of mainly processed eat out type fast foods will have bodies that are very acidic with their pineal gland becoming highly calcified and unable to work.

As our bodies age, we gather more toxins in our bodies, unless we take steps to remove these toxins our pineal gland loses much, if not all of its functions, fortunately, however, it can be resuscitated back into full health through detoxification and having the correct diet without chemical additives and manmade substitutes.

Some would suggest that a total abstinence from everything except what is in the third eye diet is to be strictly followed others suggest that a bit of leeway is to be permitted. The reality is, the less food you consume that has a negative affect the easier it is to open the third eye and the more food you eat that benefits the pineal gland the quicker and easier it will become. Once you become familiar with using your third eye you will naturally be able to determine what foods and substance you should avoid and which you want or need to consume.

To become ready to open your third eye a vegan or an only plant-based type is recommended for 2 weeks before starting to prepare your body mind and pineal gland.

Foods to Avoid

Almost everything that is manmade should be avoided; this is because it is almost always stripped of any natural goodness it once possessed while being processed. Even foods that started being "organic" when processed are changed by the process of being heated, concentrated, dried, frozen, stored and otherwise handled. They usually have artificial color, flavor and preservatives added. With the many compounds added to most household and body care products, you should not put anything on your skin that you would not eat.

Some of the commonly consumed foods and substances that should be avoided because they hinder the development and use of the Pineal Gland are:

Tobacco and Alcohol

If you want your pineal gland to thrive and function well, smoking tobacco should be avoided entirely, this includes any contact or the frequent inhalation of secondhand smoke because this can be injurious to your pineal gland. (It is also wise to avoid any smoke from open fires or cooking fires). If you come into contact with smoke and cannot avoid it, one of the best remedies is to eat parsley either fresh or dried.

Parsley contains flavonoids, apiin, apigenin, crisoeriol, and luteolin, essential oils myristicin, limonene, eugenol, and alpha-thujene. These volatile oils, qualify parsley as a chemoprotective food, claiming that it can help stabalize carcinogens, like benzopyrenes that are found in cigarette and charcoal smoke.

Having the occasional drink at a social event is considered acceptable by many people who use their third eye because it helps people to relax and become open, but should be limited to only several glasses or if you drink more, do so only on rare occasions. Using alcohol in cooking in a responsible way is usually acceptable as the alcohol is burnt off with heat, although you should be aware that most alcoholic beverages contain large amounts of sugar which is detrimental.

Many people who teach how to use the third eye would disagree and say that alcohol should be totally avoided as it disrupts the mind and concentration, but it is really up to personal choice and experience.

After being exposed to toxins from cigarettes and alcohol, having a walk in the fresh air, especially a breeze near the sea or a large body of water helps to remove toxins, this is because the air off the ocean has a negative charge; drinking pure, fresh water also helps.

Coffee and Black Tea with the active ingredient Caffeine

This is another food that its use is up for debate, there is one group of people who argue that it is detrimental to building mystic abilities and that is most probably correct when you first start to open your third eye, but once you have begun to explore the new world that has opened for you, through your third eye, many experts say that caffeine increases mystic ability by making the mind more alert and able to focus. So it is really up to the individual to decide and experiment for themselves once they have already begun.

Mercury

Unfortunately, some mercury is found in almost every type of fish, but luckily in most fish, it is not in amounts that are harmful. The fish to avoid are pilot whales, shark, large tuna, king mackerel, orange roughy swordfish and any other large predatory fish. This is because most fish except these contain selenium in amounts that effectively have a protective effect, neutralizing the mercury content making it relatively harmless.

Most processed foods

Processed foods should be avoided because of the way processing destroys many of the beneficial compounds and nutrients in the food during the processing. They are also usually made using chemically raised bulk produce as well as containing dietary hormones that are common in almost all factory farmed livestock, including beef lamb pork chicken and other poultry including farmed seafood's. The processing causes most food to be acidic and sterile

Refined sugar and Artificial Sweeteners

This includes Acesulfame potassium or Sunett, Sweet One, Aspartame or Equal, Netame, Saccharin or Sugar Twin, Sweet 'N Low, Sucralose or Splenda as well as any other added sweetener

Meat and Animal Products

Studies have revealed that people who eat only a plant-based diet have a higher level of intuitive abilities because consuming meat, especially red meat and other animal products it has been found to block or reduce the function of your pineal gland.

One theory of why you should avoid eating meat is that when an animal is stressed, hurt maimed or killed it naturally releases toxins into its body. These toxins remain in their meat, and when you consume the meat you also ingest all the toxins they contain.

Animals that are bred or lived in confined spaces such as factory farms are fed and/or injected with antibiotics, growth hormones and stimulants, fed on chemical laden foods and also subject to huge amounts of stress without the cleansing benefits of natural light fresh air and their natural foods. This cocktail of human induced compounds from these animals can not only disrupt your overall physical health but have an inhibiting effect on your mental health and in particular the pineal gland.

Pollution

Our world is filled with many kinds of pollution, whether in the form of air, land or water pollution as well as noise pollution when your ears, and mind, are attacked by loud, repetitive sounds and annoying screeching noises. Light pollution, visual pollution, thermal pollution and Internal pollution, both physical (from food) and of the mind or psyche.

We should all strive to find a place in our world where we can be away from as many types of pollution as possible in order for our third eye to develop unhindered.

Ways to Decalcify your Pineal Gland

Almost everyone has been exposed to fluoride in one form or another unless they have taken careful steps to prevent contact, so your pineal gland will have some degree of calcification. One of the best ways to decalcify is by eating Tamarind Fruit it is an extremely effective way of removing fluoride from the body. A recent study found that when children were given tamarind, they released significantly higher levels of fluoride into their urine when compared to those in the control group. Consuming tamarind can halt or even reverse the effects of skeletal fluorosis. Another good place to find natural iodine is in seaweed.

Vitamin K is also an extremely powerful detoxifier, Vitamin K1 is found in green leafy vegetables, while Vitamin K2 is created by microflora in the intestines, it can also be found in chicken or goose livers, egg yolks, organic dairy, fermented vegetables and shellfish. In combination with Vitamin A and D it can detoxify and help to remove calcium from the pineal gland and arteries, transferring it to the bones, where it is known to do the most good.

Chapter 9: Frequently Asked Questions

Even though you now have a basic knowledge of what the third eye is and what it can do, you may find that you have a few more questions that have not been discussed yet. In this section, we'll go over some of the most common FAQs regarding the third eye, to deepen your understanding and clear things up before you move on to the practices that will help you open the third eye.

How will I know my third eye is open?

You will know that your third eye is open when you have real experiences that indicate its activation. When your third eye is awake, you will find yourself aware of things before they happen. You may be thinking of someone, just before they call or text you. You may get a terrible feeling, just before receiving news that someone has been harmed. You may also feel a pull toward a particular person or place, only to find that pursuing this feeling moves you closer toward your goals.

Sometimes, the opening of your third eye is not as apparent. Even if you are aware of the world around you, the information traded between the pineal gland and your mind is a two-way street. You must also be receptive to the signals being sent out from the third eye to your mind. Pay attention to the cues that your mind is sending, and you will find yourself better prepared for receiving these signals.

What is the easiest way to open the third eye?

If you look to the lifestyles of Buddhists, Taoists, and other groups, you will see that many of them place heavy emphasis on meditation. As people continue to neglect the third eye, it can develop calcification that makes it harder to open. Meditation helps remove this calcification. You do not need tarot cards or a crystal ball to achieve it—you just need to focus your energy inward and set your mind toward opening the third eye.

Can anyone open the third eye?

Earlier in this book, it was mentioned that everyone has access to this third eye. That is true to an extent. Yes, everyone who has a pineal gland can open their third eye. However, the pineal gland is sometimes missing from children who have not yet reached the age of 7. Those suffering from mental disorders or who are mentally disabled also may not be able to create the bridge between the mind and body that is necessary to connect with the third eye.

Is there a 'zone' where opening the third eye will become effortless?

Interestingly enough, the third eye is something that requires relaxation with intention, rather than focus. If you try too hard to connect to the third eye, you can end up inhibiting your efforts. This could be one of the reasons that people who promote relaxation through meditation are the most successful in creating that critical link between their mind and body that is necessary to be receptive to the signals sent out by the third eye.

Even so, there may come a time when you are relaxed in your way of life. Stresses will have melted away because you are confident that your third eye will help you find the path that is most likely to help you find success and happiness. This relaxation will create a 'zone' where it seems you are constantly and effortlessly connected to the third eye. This is a guidance that you achieve without effort, and you will likely feel connected to all things in life. Once you have reached this zone once, feel confident that you have broken down the calcification around your third eye and know that it will happen more easily in the future.

How long will it take me to open the third eye?

Your ability to open the third eye has a lot to do with your personal spirituality and how much you trust your mind. Some people are also closer to consciously opening the third eye than others because of their life practices. Even so, few people ever open their third eye 100% over the course of their lifetime. Instead of focusing on an end goal of completely activating your eye, focus on the continued betterment of your skillset.

Can I learn to astral project, speak to ghosts, read auras, or see into the future?

People with questions like these often expect to be gifted powers from the third eye. Frequently, skills like these are referred to as 'natures' of the third eye. Some people learn to read auras or astral project, while others only experience greater intuition and heightened purpose in life. You may find that you are predisposed to one of these skills.

Otherwise, it could take years or longer to learn one of these skills. If you are trying to learn a specific skill without progress, it might be useful to seek a teacher that is knowledgeable in the specific area.

What is going to happen when I open my third eye?

The experience of opening the third eye often feels like a deep vibration from inside your mind. You may also see a blue ball of light if you are trying to create the energy while meditating. In your day-to-day activities, you will notice that you are able to make decisions, based on instinct, that later work out to be true. You may also feel as if your actions have become more purposeful.

Should I tell my family and friends about my newfound enlightenment?

There is a lot of stigma surrounding the third eye and the heightened consciousness that goes along with it. Some may misunderstand the third eye and call it evil, while others will leave it up to tricks of your mind. It can be exciting once you form that connection and even more exciting to share your experience with people who might learn something from it. However, that does not mean that you should start discussing your heightened experience with everyone you meet.

As strong as your mind may be, it is very easy to be discouraged by the words of others. You cannot possibly expect to create that connection between the third eye, body, and mind that is necessary to experience the insight of the third eye with doubt in your mind. Speaking to others before you are confident in your abilities might cause a setback, and even deter you from your goal altogether. If you do choose to share, do it among those who are least likely to judge you. Choose your audience wisely and share with people who will support this enlightenment instead of belittling it.

Do I need a teacher to learn about the third eye?

Some people look for the guidance of a teacher as they try to open the third eye, determined to make their experience worthwhile. Having a teacher has its benefits, especially for people who learn better through one-on-one interaction and watching others. However, you do not necessarily need a teacher to open your third eye. Many people have trouble finding authentic practitioners in this area, and someone who is committed enough can learn to open their third eye on their own.

Can other people notice when my third eye is open?

The experience of the third eye is an overlay with your own senses. You 'see' things if you see them because your third eye is interacting with your eyes. When you get a feeling in your gut, it is the third eye interacting with the physical sensations you are experiencing. The exception is if you are deeply immersed in your connection to the third eye and seem distracted. Then, it might seem like you are not paying attention to them, but they still will not physically see anything you are experiencing.

Why is opening the third eye more difficult or impossible around certain people?

Something that should always remember is that the third eye represents possibilities. The third eye detects that this person does not believe that ability and will not open. If the person you are with is not open to the possibilities, then the connection cannot be created, and you cannot share information with them. This happens because judgment clouds perception and makes it difficult to accept things as they are, without labeling them or framing them a certain way. If the other person is judging the abilities of the third eye, the third eye becomes clouded.

Is the third eye evil?

One of the reasons that people judge those who aim to open their third eye is because some people view it as being 'evil' or 'bad'. Something that is important to remember is that nothing is inherently 'good' or 'evil'. These are not a state of being, but the collective personal choices that we make. It is the actions that we take that make something good or evil—the very same knife that prepares a wonderful meal to feed a homeless population could be used to kill a man—it just depends on how that knife is used.

The third eye is as good or evil as anything else—what truly matters is the way that you use it. Do not corrupt your nature and do not use the third eye with the intent of causing harm. If it feels 'bad', then don't do it. By following these simple rules, you can make decisions using your third eye that feel good.

Could I connect with dangerous things when opening the third eye?

It is not uncommon for people unfamiliar with the third eye to be fearful of the things that they might 'see' when opening it. Some people may communicate with spirits, which Hollywood has turned into a very dangerous happening. However, it's important to keep in mind that you are not going to connect to your third eye and experience the pouring of spirits from some unknown realm. A significant part of the experience is what you are willing to accept, so ultimately, you are in control of the nature that you pursue with your third eye. There might be some small risk, but that often happens when people make the choice to use the third eye to reach out to darker, more dangerous entities.

The only other threat is from delusion. Delusion happens when people force the third eye opening, believing that they are having an experience or seeing something that is not really there. This might cause them to act out in ways that they wouldn't otherwise. By preparing your mind in the right way, as you will learn about in the next section of the book, delusion becomes less likely.

Is the third eye spiritual?

The third eye does have many spiritual implications—it is even mentioned in many of the religions around the world. The third eye is spiritual to an extent, in the sense that at a bare minimum, you must be in touch with your own spirit and the flow of your own energy in the world. This does not mean that you cannot open the third eye if you are not spiritual—but don't be surprised if the meditation and other practices take you to a deeper place within yourself. If you are successful at opening the third eye, then you will find yourself with a new spirituality as well.

Is the third eye anti-Christian?

Even though the Bible mentions the third eye and how it has implications for both good and evil, it is generally considered against the Christian religion. According to the principles of Christianity, the third eye is not of God. Some other mentions in the Bible include the idea that those with third eye powers are either deceiving themselves and others or under the influence of a demonic force. It is said that consulting with mediums and psychics goes against God. In the Old Testament, it was reported that acting as a psychic or medium was punishable by death.

The sixth sense that is supported under Christian philosophies is the idea of the Holy Spirit as the sixth sense. It is said that it is the Holy Spirit that should teach truth and guide people in life.

Chapter 10: Techniques For Effective Meditation

1. Always make observations.

Those who call themselves wallflowers think that they have better intuitive understanding of the surroundings compared to most people. They might just be right simply because these people are the ones who are more inclined to listening and observing others. Because of this, they can understand more and see through body languages, expressions and other forms of inexplicit cues. These people tend to become better at detecting lies, read through sarcasm and other indirect or subtle messages.

One can become a better observer in so many ways. You can try going to the nearby park or at a coffee shop and observe people. Listen to their conversations without being intrusive or rude. Concoct your own story based on these conversations, such as how they knew each other and any other information you could think. The more often you do this, the better observer you become.

The next time you ride a public transit, observe other passengers and what they do while waiting to arrive at their destination, whether they are reading a book, a newspaper, doing nothing, listening to music, and so on. Also, when you get to sit around the table with friends, start observing and be quiet for some time. Just listen to your friends as they exchange words and watch how they react to a statement or observe your friends to what they are thinking when they're listening. Again, the more you do this, the better observer you become.

2. Observe your dreams

Individuals who have psychic powers think that some dreams may be premonitions. But before you can analyze and make conclusions, you have to pay attention to what your dreams are. Start writing down your dreams and keep track of possible patterns or connections that may lead you to a significant information or answer. Have a dream diary and always keep it beside you when you sleep so that when you wake up, you can write your dreams immediately. Most often, we forget our dreams within the day. Only a few of these are retained in our memories, so always write them down after waking up.

3. Pay attention to your gut feel

We all have a gut feel about different people, places and events which are hard to explain. You probably had the instinct that something strange is going to happen without any supporting evidence or any other instances that led you to think so. This gut feel is often overlooked by people and instead opt to make rational judgments. Next time when you have a gut feel of a certain event, write it down for you to read later on and see if it happens in reality. Also notice how your gut feel connect to yourself. However, you should also remember that not all gut feels could be true, or if it is true, it may not unravel immediately in your life. The best thing to do is to write it down and get back to it later.

Chapter 11: Opening The Indigo Chakra

New Age practitioners believe that aside from activating your pineal gland, which is your physical third eye, you have to enhance your true third eye, the indigo chakra.

We will briefly discuss the indigo chakra in this chapter.

The Significance of the Color Indigo
You have learned that the indigo chakra is responsible in opening your subconscious and bringing you to a higher level of awareness of the spirit world. Indigo is also referred to as royal blue color. This color symbolizes deep inner knowing and infinite wisdom.

Indigo enables you to connect to the Divine. Indigo is also associated with the color of the night. It is said that it is at nighttime that your senses are finer and an inner part of you is easy to awaken.

The color indigo is perceived to bring clarity to your senses – hearing, seeing, and feeling. This is also associated with the third eye.

Indigo is the color of deep change energy. Experts say that if you are able to open your indigo chakra, you are likely to experience a lot of **Aha!** moments – which are moments of complete clarity and wise insight. You will begin to recognize different patterns and will be able to relate them to the bigger picture.

Opening your indigo chakra leads you to consciously live your life – gives you the control over your future.

Physical Aspect of the Indigo Chakra
The indigo chakra is located at the center of your forehead, above your brow. It is associated with the brain, the pituitary gland, pineal gland, carotid nerve plexus, your eyes, and nose. Those who possess strong indigo energy are said to have a unique spark in their eyes. They possess a sense of deep wisdom and you can feel

that when you look straight into their eyes. You feel the calmness but there is still a feeling of strong energy, which can transform and change anybody.

If you have a strong indigo chakra, you have a healthy thyroid gland, you have good vision, you don't encounter problems in your metabolism, you have a flexible neck, you possess good oral health, and you have remarkable upper body strength.

Mental Aspect of the Indigo Chakra

Indigo is also a symbol of deep thinking. It represents the path to **effortless action;** meaning your actions do not impose on your ego and on your situation. Your actions just flow through and you accomplish anything with much effort.

If you have a strong indigo chakra, you have excellent memory, you can recall your dreams, you can easily visualize, and you have excellent mental strength.

Emotional Aspect of the Indigo Chakra
Indigo is similar to blue, the color of peace and tranquility. If your indigo chakra is open, you can easily achieve peace within yourself and it is manifested in your own life. You know that everything is in place and that there is nothing you have to change. All is well and you believe that everything that happens to you comes from the Divine.

You only experience chaos when the indigo chakra is blocked by depression, sadness, loneliness, and hallucinations.

When your indigo chakra is strong, you are perceptive, intuitive, sensitive, you are comfortable with any psychic experiences, you are emotionally balanced, and generally peaceful.

Spiritual Aspect of the Indigo Chakra
The spiritual aspect of indigo is your ability to believe that everything that is happening in your life is the workings of the Divine.

If your indigo chakra is strong you are said to be full of wisdom. You are clairvoyant and you are united with the state of consciousness. You have mystical experiences and you don't question them. You also have the ability to see both the inner and outer truths. You have strong spiritual will and you have an excellent ability to transcend polarity.

Sixth Sense
Inner voice, gut feel, intuition, or sixth sense – it is always available because it is a natural process of your subconscious, you just don't utilize it more often. When you indigo chakra is cleansed, you are able to connect more to your sixth sense.

Activating Your Indigo Chakra
To completely open your indigo chakra, there has to be a balance between all the other chakras. (Now that is for another discussion.)

Here are some of the ways that you can activate your indigo chakra:

- It is activated by understanding and accepting your own self – your weaknesses and your strengths.

- Begin to understand that the other person you are looking at is a manifestation of yourself. It is the realization that every human being belongs to a **unified whole.**

- You have to work on how to be one with the universe.

Chapter 12: Divert Energy To The Third Eye

If a third eye chakra is not working properly, that could mean it's not receiving enough energy. Remember that the chakra system is made up of seven main energy centers, or chakras. Each is individually responsible for its own spiritual, mental and physical manifestations of health.

A properly-aligned chakra system means that energy is flowing at full capacity through each chakra. You are firing on all cylinders, and your health and success all seem to be in place. The problem with energy is that it is fluid and constantly changing. This may mean that your chakras become imbalanced very easily, and it is necessary to maintain a decent balance so that you may continue to reap the benefits.

When your life is feeling aimless and off-track, one of the possible reasons is that your chakras are off balance, but it is most likely related to your third eye. During times like this, it is necessary to divert some energy from your other chakras to share with the third eye to restore the balance.

Once things begin to make sense again, this means you have successfully balanced your chakra. You begin to feel a purpose for your everyday activities, a vision of what you want your future to look like, and a general enthusiasm that wasn't there before. Should you unlock its full potential, it is even possible to develop clairvoyant abilities through your third eye.

One study estimated that between fifty and seventy-five percent of adults have a calcified pineal gland, yet it rarely occurs under the age of twelve. Consider the differences in thought processes between an adult and a child. We see stories and videos of children with endless compassion and empathy. They also have amazing talents and the capacity to love unconditionally. They have boundless energy and are always up for new and exciting things. Is the process of calcification eliminating our human qualities as we age? Is it possible to get it back?

Do you remember the causes of a blocked third eye that we have discussed? We must also consider that energy is being sucked from us by our environment. Living or working in environments that are largely negative is a common source of third eye blockages. Dealing with difficult or exhausting people often literally sucks the energy right out of you.

While it may not be possible to remove yourself completely, it is possible to protect yourself. The old idea of staying out of drama and avoiding problems that are not your own (problems that you don't have the capacity to solve) is a great way to keep your third eye energy up.

People that are, for better or worse, highly affected by outside energy are called 'empaths.' These people are often hypersensitive to negative energy in their surroundings, and unless they take steps to shield themselves, let that energy in, which affects their mood, outlook on life and overall well-being.

It is common practice for an empath to shield themselves from outside negativity by creating an energy barrier, sort of like a force field, in order to maintain their positive energy. Think of it as an aura of light around you, which nothing can penetrate. You too can create such an aura by first imagining that it is there and making the conscious choice to not let outside influences affect your well-being. Choose not to get annoyed by morning traffic, don't allow stress about work to ruin your flow, and certainly don't get caught up in any office drama.

Be vigilant of the energy that surrounds you and combat it with your positive light. Even a tiny speck of light is visible in the dark, and light conquers the darkness every time. Instead of letting it take over you, make the choice to shine your bright light and bring some positivity into your situation. Maybe you're not currently on your true path, but consider that the lessons you learn here will prepare you for your calling. Take each lesson with patience and gratitude, and you will be rewarded for it in the future.

If you feel like your energy has been drained, you have to take the necessary steps to get it back. Pulling in new energy is a great way to do that. There are many meditative practices available to help you tap into the universal energy and draw its positive light toward you. Doing so flushes your chakra system with new energy, unblocks energy flow, and realigns your system.

It is also possible to pull energy from chakras that are getting too much energy and transfer it to the third eye chakra. It is certainly possible that one chakra can receive too much energy, especially if the rest is blocked. Too much energy can lead to problems like anxiety or overcompensation in physical ailments.

The first step in diverting energy is accepting the notion that the third eye exists. As we have discussed before, our modern society has cast aside the existence of spiritual centers for modern technology and medicine. Most people have not even heard of the third eye or chakra system, and therefore, don't believe it exists. This lack of awareness drains energy from the chakra, just when it needs it most.

Improving the health of your third eye will take practice. One of the best ways to do this is with regular meditation accompanied by learning how to rely on your third eye in everyday life. Meditation can help you get in touch with your inner self through the use of your third eye. Instead of leaving this meditative state when you are finished, carry the notion of your third eye with you throughout the day. Get used to relying on its guidance to make even the simplest decisions. Practicing recognition of its cues makes it stronger and more effective. Giving it the attention it deserves transfers energy to it and amplifies its effects.

Expect some side effects. Once you begin listening to the guidance of your third eye, things will start to change. Perhaps you regularly stretch yourself too thin, and your inner self is guiding you to let go of some of your responsibilities. This may mean you cannot drive carpool every day or bend over backward to appease your boss. You only have so much energy and it is necessary to pool it for the things that truly matter to you. This may mean disappointing or inconveniencing others, but in time, things will work out the way they are supposed to.

Just remember that this adjustment can feel difficult, but it is necessary to put you back on the right track. Imagine two paths running parallel in the middle of a dense forest. Through the trees, you can catch small glimpses of the path to your right. The light that shines through the trees onto that path draws you in, and you imagine how warm that sunshine will feel on your shoulders.

The paths do not converge but run parallel endlessly. Your choice is to stay on the path you are currently on because it's easy, and bound to get you somewhere. The other option is to brave the forest, its dangers, and the darkness to get to the other trail. You are bound to get hurt and you can even lose your way, but on the other side is that warm, familiar path that you've always dreamed of reaching.

Chapter 13: Interacting With The Third Eye

Once you have gone through the process of opening your third eye, it is important that you begin to put it to good use. In a way, opening your third eye is like learning another language. If you had another language at your disposal, you would want to go out and use it as often as possible. You would find places where the people spoke that language, watch TV shows in that language, and generally do whatever you could to hone your skills and become more fluent. This is precisely what you want to do with your third eye skills. This chapter will present several ways in which you can interact with your third eye, thereby strengthening it while also developing new skills that you can apply to your day-to-day life.

Opening your Mind

The impact that the third eye has on imagination and visualization cannot be overstated. In short, people with little to no imagination probably have underperforming pineal glands. However, once you have awakened your third eye, you will begin to experience a wealth of thoughts, ideas, and images in your mind, bringing a whole new level of imagination to your life. At first, you might not know what to do with this newfound source of images and ideas, but with a little practice, you can find ways to enrich your life with the material it offers.

Your imagination will become clearer, richer and more readily available once your third eye is opened. The trick is to use your imagination as often as possible in order to maintain good third eye health. One way to do this is to start solving problems by thinking outside the box. This term is used to describe someone who doesn't rely on traditional solutions for problems. When you begin to imagine solutions you will find ideas that others never considered. Not only will these ideas prove to be the best ones for the situation at hand, but they will also create opportunities for other imaginative ideas to be put to use. In the end, you will be respected for your ability to conjure up solutions that most people would never have thought of.

Another good practice is to study symbols and their meanings. Symbols are used to evoke emotional responses within a person, that's why they are as effective as they are. Religious symbols, for example, will convey deep and rich messages without using a single word. This form of communication relies heavily on an active and healthy third eye. Those lacking insight will only see the physical image and nothing more. However, when your third eye is opened, you will be able to gain insight and meaning into symbols you have never seen before. This is virtually like learning another language, except you will find that you already understand it without having to try.

Tapping into Divine Wisdom

Another form of this spiritual language is divination. At first glance you might be tempted to scoff at the notion of divination, seeing it as a scam where people charge money to tell of things that may or may not come true. Unfortunately, this is a common problem, one that paints a very negative picture on divination in general. However, there is a very real and sacred side to divination, one that practitioners know very well. Once you have opened your third eye, you will begin to experience this phenomenon whether you believe in it or not.

The reason for this is that true divination is an extension of intuition. Since the third eye allows you to tap into divine wisdom, you already have access to information beyond what your physical senses can provide. Any form of divination will serve to present that intuition in a tangible way. It will act as a tool that projects intuition into the physical world. Tarot cards don't know what the future holds, but your intuition does, and it's that intuition that directs which cards are drawn. This is the true nature of divination. It is the physical communication between your intuitive mind and your conscious mind.

The trick is to find a form of divination that works for you. While all forms of divination have the potential to serve the same function, they won't necessarily provide the same experience for the user. Some people do better with cards, be they Tarot cards, playing cards or some other type. Others find using small objects like coins, runes or the like provide a more meaningful and reliable experience. The important thing to remember is that there is no shame in trying several forms before finding the one that works for you. Once you find your divination style, you will be able to find answers to just about any question with great skill, accuracy, and ease.

Dreams, Lucid Dreams, and Otherworldly Experiences

Another way to interact with the third eye is to use it as the gateway between worlds that it is. You can either use it to transfer your subconscious into the physical world, as in the case of dreams, or you can use it to transfer your conscious mind into the spiritual world, as in the case of lucid dreams and otherworldly experiences such as astral projection. An open third eye will increase the quantity and quality of your dreams, providing you with a wonderful experience each and every night while you sleep. Some of these dreams will be products of your newfound imagination, creating an experience that is entertaining and thrilling. Others, however, can be the result of your heightened intuition. Such dreams will often prove to be prophetic, giving you insight into an event, meeting or experience yet to unfold. A great way to improve the proficiency of your dreams is to keep a dream journal in which you record your dreamtime experiences.

Lucid dreams are those in which you become aware that you are dreaming. The ability to awaken within a dream gives you the opportunity to explore the dream world with purpose and intention, rather than simply allowing your dreams to take you wherever they want. Furthermore, you can actually create the dream you are having once you become lucid. You can choose to fly to exotic and faraway locations, talk to famous people, chill out on a tropical island or do anything that your mind can conceive. The better you become at lucid dreaming, the richer and more exciting your lucid dreams will become. In many ancient traditions, as well as several modern ones, lucid dreaming was seen as a conscious experience in the spirit world, one that has infinite possibilities.

Astral travel is one example of an otherworldly experience you can have once your third eye is open and strong. This is a similar experience to lucid dreaming, except that it takes place in the physical world. In other words, your conscious mind exits your body and becomes present elsewhere while awake. Numerous accounts report people being able to detect if not actually see the person's astral body in such cases; however, it seems that the astral image is usually invisible. This could be connected to whether the other people present have their third eye open or not. However, when your third eye is open, you will be able to explore such otherworldly phenomena. Astral projection is not an easy skill to develop, but it is one that proves well worth the time and effort required.

Chapter 14: Meditation Techniques

Getting in touch with your third eye can be as simple as meditating daily. If you are not familiar with the ideas behind meditation, it may seem a bit far-fetched. How could sitting quietly in a comfortable room possibly do me any good when I have so many other things to do?

Perhaps you are so busy because you have yet to meditate. The overwhelming feelings of the day often come from having lots to do but also trying to get them done with a mind that is already at full capacity. Would that same list of tasks somehow seem easier if your mind was clear and focused?

Meditation should not be intimidating. We often see people who meditate and reach a whole other plane of thinking during their sessions. They devote hours and hours to practice each day and somehow are still capable of taking part in normal society. Either that, or they are Buddhist monks who live in the Himalayas, but either way they still got some work done.

The good news is, everyone is good at meditation, as this is an individual practice. Every person will have their own interpretation of their results, and the only goal is to calm the mind and create inner peace. Silencing the mind makes room for the third eye to speak up and be heard.

This does not happen overnight. You simply cannot meditate once and become enlightened, all-knowing, and on your path to true happiness. Meditation practice is just that, practice. Each and every time, you will receive exactly what you are meant to receive.

In small doses, you will gain understanding and insight into the problems you face. You will begin to see patterns and understand how to connect past problems and their solutions with your current situation. You are simply stopping to think your way through, instead of continuing on making decisions aimlessly. Think of meditation as taking a daily multivitamin for your spirit.

There are many different types of meditation and finding what is right for you will take a little bit of time and experimentation. You may find that certain practices allow you to focus your mind quickly, while others prove to be less satisfying. Over time, you may change your tune and like something else. Just like energy, meditation practice is fluid and up for debate. You do not need to permanently settle on something.

That being said, let's talk about some of the options. Take a look at the different types of meditation and try whatever it is that stands out to you. Feel free to change your mind.

Guided imagery

If you are new to meditation, trying a practice like 'guided imagery' could be a good place to start. People who are new to meditation will likely have a hard time focusing the mind. They will often drift off to random thoughts that eventually consume their mind, instead of passively letting them go.

Guided imagery usually involves some type of audio or visual prompt. Sitting quietly, the meditator is asked to envision a scene in their head. This could be a quiet meadow, a calm beach, or anything relaxing ideally. They are asked to imagine each and every detail, down to the scent of the grass, the feeling of the sunshine on their face, and the sound of birds chirping in the background.

This imagery gives the mind something to focus on, other than the problems they are trying to escape. The imagery brings feelings of calm and relaxation and gives the brain time to reboot before switching back to problem-solving mode.

Interestingly enough, this method is so effective that it is often used as a therapeutic way to treat mental disorders like anxiety and depression. A trained practitioner can help a patient imagine the specific situation that gives them anxiety and help soothe them to get over that anxiety without ever leaving the office. This is very powerful stuff.

Mindfulness

This is a relatively new offshoot of meditation, and it's recommended for beginners who want to practice meditating. This practice is simply the act of being aware of yourself, inside and out. Begin by taking a comfortable position and steadying your breath. You are aware of your own breathing, as you slowly and deeply breathe in then slowly and steadily breathe out. You can imagine the flow of energy coursing through you.

Imagine feeling it in your fingers and toes, surrounding your heart, your liver, and kidneys. Imagine it bringing fresh energy to what ails you. If your back hurts, focus a great deal of energy there. If you feel your third eye chakra needs some love, send the energy right between the eyes, and feel it tingle as it takes hold.

Again, this type of meditation gives the mind something to focus on, which makes it more likely that your thoughts will stay on this task instead of slipping back to that problem you had at work.

Passive

There are many types of passive meditation, in which the practitioner simply sits quietly and lets their thoughts enter and leave as they may. The trick here is to simply acknowledge that the thought is there, but not assigning any value to it.

For example, if you think about driving the kids to soccer practice in an hour, you simply allow that thought to float in, and back out. Be above any additional considerations. Don't think about getting the kids dressed and ready, about where you should park, or who you might run into. Just simply see the thought, compartmentalize it, and send it on its way.

This type of meditation is a little more difficult and takes more focus to master. However, this method requires no outside help as with guided imagery. It is also highly variable by the type of thoughts you decide to have during that time, but meditating with your thoughts at the ready can also be very helpful in solving problems. Some people have great epiphanies during meditation and manage to solve the problems they have been trying to solve for a long time.

There are a number of other active forms of meditation, like 'Transcendental,' 'Kundalini,' and 'Heart Rhythm Meditation.' Each of these asks you to focus on different aspects of your internal energy as it relates to that of the universe. You can choose to focus on your breath, match it to the rhythm of your heartbeat, and imagine the energy coursing through you. Each has its benefits, and you can choose whatever you want depending on your personal preference.

All forms of meditation have things in common, so even if you don't know where you want to start, some things are clear. The goal is to quiet your mind, so finding a quiet spot in your home or office to practice is a great start. There doesn't have to be a goal or endpoint to meditation, so simply sitting comfortably and in silence it a great way to get started.

Instead of committing yourself to a specific practice, simply sit quietly, eyes closed, and see where your mind takes you. For a few minutes, allow your thoughts to filter in and out. This will happen naturally and is virtually impossible to stop. Don't get frustrated if a thought pops in. Just let it be, and watch it float on by.

Practice utter emptiness next. Try your best to clear the mind of all thoughts and focus on one thing exclusively. Perhaps this is a sound, like a gong, or an image, or even feeling. Focus your attention on whatever it is and continually bring your mind back to it as it decides to wander.

If you are new to meditation, you probably won't be good at these tasks at first. That is why we should practice. Over time, you will have a greater ability to focus on the task at hand during meditation, and this skill will carry through to the rest of your life. Focus during meditation means you are practicing skills that will help you focus on tasks, increasing mental acuity in your daily life.

Chapter 15: Using Guided Meditation To Awaken Your Higher Self

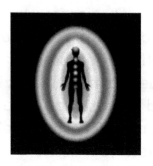

You may already meditate and take advantage of the benefits. If not, learning about the technique can aid you in reaching higher consciousness. When you are meditating, you are focusing your attention on a single thing. This might be a thought or phrase, a sense or sensation or your breath. The point is to get away from the distracting and negative thoughts that are creeping into your life and causing issues. With regular practice of meditation, it is possible to focus on the present and the exact moment that you are in.

There are multiple types of meditation. Guided meditation is ideal for all people, but especially beginners. It essentially gives you a road map so that you can focus on the benefits of your sessions instead of the technique and mechanics. It is referred to as guided because you have a trained meditation professional essentially helping you to navigate your sessions. This might be in perform or in the form of a sound recording, audiovisual media, written text or a video.

With guided meditation, it is common for an element of visualization to be involved in the process. This can be used to recreate or simulate sensory perception of different tastes, movements, smells, sights and sounds.

Your mind and mental health are one of the most common reasons why someone might engage in meditation. Studies have been done to show the different benefits of this practice. One research study that was conducted in 2012 looked at 50 people who never meditate and another 50 who do. The study concluded that those with years of meditation experience have more outer layer brain folds. This phenomenon may make it easier for the brain to process information. When you are able to more effectively process information, it makes it easier to learn, solve problems and cope with stress.

Aging can have a number of effects on the brain. Three studies were reviewed in 2013 that looked at how meditation might affect this. The reviewers state that normal age-related brain changes may be slowed, reversed or stalled when someone practices meditation on a regular basis.

There are other effects related to mental and emotional health that might be beneficial among those who practice meditation regularly. These can include:

- Reducing your overall stress levels

- Helping you to gain greater control over your anxiety
- Aiding in promoting a better sense of total emotional health
- Improving your ability to be self-aware
- Helping to give you a longer and more controlled attention span
- Reducing the risk of memory loss, especially when it is associated with aging
- Aiding those who are trying to overcome an addiction

In addition to healing the mind and achieving greater mindfulness, someone might also opt to meditate to improve their physical well-being. Like the mental effects, several studies have been done exploring how regular practice might contribute to a greater level of mental health. The following may be helped by meditation:

- Pain

- Irritable bowel syndrome
- Insomnia
- High blood pressure
- Ulcerative colitis
- Smoking cessation

While guided meditation is one of the most popular, it is far from the only technique to consider. There are seven others to learn about that have various benefits. As you are exploring these, take a few minutes to think about what you hope to achieve from meditation. This will make it easier to choose which technique is the most ideal. Remember that you can also choose to utilize multiple types of meditation. If you do this, ensure that there is a balance of the techniques that you are utilizing so that you are able to reap the most benefit from all. These seven include:

- Transcendental meditation is used by those seeking to get to a state of enlightenment. It combines chanting a mantra, sitting in the Lotus position and putting your focus on getting above the negativity in your life. This is often learned at different meditation retreats. It is best to learn from an expert so that you can ensure that you are doing it properly.

- Heart rhythm meditation is focused on developing your consciousness. It is a type of downward meditation. As the name implies, the heart is where this meditation form is concentrated. You will repeat a mantra as you go through the process. When you do this type regularly, it allows you to find a deeper level of joy while also improving your ability to handle stress.

- Guided visualization is used for stress relief, spiritual healing and personal development. Buddha is the inspiration for this type of meditation. What you become is due to what you think. This type looks at the mind being everything. You will spend time imagining experiences that are positive and relaxing. Positive feelings are then generated due to the chemicals that your body releases during the meditation process. You can choose to put in a lot of focus or use this meditation type in a more casual way.

- Kundalini looks at rising streams of energy and it is considered to be a type of upward meditation. It has both Hindu and Buddhist roots. While it is used for its healing benefits, it is also believed to be somewhat metaphoric. Those practicing it may experience altered consciousness once they feel the energy.

- Zazen is a type of seated meditation. You use self-guidance so it is relatively easy to use. The purpose is to rid yourself of all of the various judgmental ideas, images and thoughts that you are experiencing.

- Qigong works to promote relaxation while also improving respiration and posture. When looking at all forms of meditation, this is one of the oldest.

You will use movement, breathing techniques and meditation together.

- Mindfulness is a type of meditation that makes it possible for you to fully acknowledge your reality. As part of the process, you are going to just let your mind wander and then consider the various thoughts that you have so that you can analyze them and understand why such thoughts are in your head in the first place.

Meditation Session #6: Mini Mindfulness Meditation – 5 Minutes

If you need a few minutes to ground yourself before a big meeting or something else causes you stress, this meditation is beneficial. Take a few minutes to close your eyes, breathe and think about the upcoming situation. Visualize it going well and push the negative thoughts from your mind. Reaffirm who you are and your strengths.

Take three more deep breaths and open
your eyes.

Chapter 16: Finding Happiness From Within

Demonstrating practices to awaken your Third Eye and align all seven chakras has numerous health, spiritual, and emotional benefits. Meditation is an exercise that cannot only energize the entire system of chakras, but it can also help you obtain a happier lifestyle that originates from within. Opening or awakening the Third Eye will bring to you a positive sense of peace and happiness that will result in your having a positive perception of the other areas of your life.

Does Meditation Result in Increased Happiness?

Many people who regularly incorporate meditation into their daily lives have claimed that since they have begun the practice of meditation they have experienced an increase in happiness in their lifestyles. How can this be true? How can doing one activity for a short period each day have an impact on your life as a whole?

There are many reasons why meditation can be explained as resulting in a general and even prolonged feeling of happiness. The first branch of explanation can be summarized as simply as stating that, by meditating, you project positive energy. In projecting and embracing more positive energy, you gain a more positive perspective overall and are able to experience greater happiness. Meditation not only allows you to see your life in a more positive manner, but it also helps you to view yourself in a more positive light. Having the ability to view yourself in a positive way will, in turn, result in increased confidence.

Third Eye Awakening asks you to focus on pushing out or completely eliminating (if possible) negative energy from your life. In eliminating the negative energy from our daily lives, we are left only with positive thoughts and positive energy. Eliminating the negative not only results in an increase in positive energy but it also greatly reduces anxiety which allows us to live happier, more relaxed lives. The way that you meditate will also greatly affect the amount of happiness that it can bring to your life. By meditating first thing in the morning, you begin each day relaxed and readier to be productive. Setting even a small portion of time each day aside for Third Eye awakening (or the alignment of all seven chakras) can enable you the chance to not only relax but to sit with your thoughts and prepare for the day ahead. Rather than waking up last minute in a panic and rushing out of the house, try to begin each morning with a short meditation session. You are guaranteed to be more relaxed and happy in your daily life if you begin the morning in a happy, stress-free state of mind.

Chapter 17: The Dark Side Of The Third Eye Chakra

Issues and Challenges: Clinging to highbrow wandering and daydreaming; attachment to "powers"; imagining and telling others that one is more enlightened than one actually is.

The poor factor of the ajna chakra can take the form of both deficiency or overexpression of its traits. Third eye chakra deficiency includes being insensitive to others, blocking off our attention in their emotions and dispositions. "In the general public this internal eye remains closed," says Swami Satyananda Saraswati, "and even though they see the events of the outdoor international, know-how and expertise of truth cannot be won. In this experience, we are unaware of the actual opportunities of the arena, unable to view the deeper degrees of human lifestyles."

It is straightforward to fall into misinterpretation or projection after a third eye chakra starting. Your biases, possibilities, and prejudices (all of us have a few) may also cause your instinct to be wrong, or reason you to attract wrong conclusions about others' meanings and reasons. Sri Aurobindo Ghose reminds us that "I am... inwardly actual to myself but the invisible lifestyles of others has first-class an indirect truth to me besides in to date because it impinges on my own thoughts, existence and senses."

To counter those ajna chakra tendencies, consider this: When you believe you studied you perceive something, take a look at it out. You can tell others what you believe you studied you're seeing, hearing, or feeling from your zero.33 eye chakra with regards to them and ask whether your perceptions are right or now not. If they're pronouncing you're now not, receive their declaration, at the least on the floor. Nothing beneficial may be received with the aid of insisting which you are right and they're incorrect. At the least, if a person says you're wrong but you're quite sure you're right, keep it on your mind as a guess, a speculation. It would possibly display beneficial or maybe critical. However, it may not, or it might be vain or motive you to behave badly.

Chapter 18: Evidence Behind The Theory Of The Third Eye

The concept of "Third Eye" is not something new. It is an age-old concept. If we flip through the pages of history, we will come across many chapters where the existence of the "Third Eye" has been mentioned time and again. You will find it in animals such as the ancient tuataras or iguanas of New Zealand. If we go by the different research studies across the generations, we can safely say that there is a high possibility that the Third eEe is nature's first eye, especially in case of the vertebrates and man. However, the mystery shrouding the role and function of the pineal gland is still not clear.

If we take the scientific explanations, then it is made up of cells that have distinct and unique features which are very similar to the light sensitive cells found in the retina. Hence, we can safely say that this organ is related to the power of sight. This gland receives signals from the brain, and gives signals to the optic nerves. This pea shaped gland secretes the hormone melatonin, which plays a significant role in the circadian rhythms or the sleep/wake cycle.

Let us consider the Theosophical literature aspect. This literature emphasizes that in addition to the physiological functions, this gland also plays an important role as the psycho-physiological center or the 6th chakra which is involved with intuition, the sixth sense.

The world of myths and mysteries are no less. They have their own explanations. They have their own concepts regarding the evolution of human civilization and the importance of the Third Eye. If you read through the story of the Ulysses fights, you will fight the mention of the one eyed giant Cyclops of Greece. In Hinduism, you will find the mention of the Third Eye as part of the mystical eye of Siva which stands for direct cosmic vision and intuition. These timeless folklores tell stories about how mankind came into existence and the different battles fought.

If we check out the writings and information collected on the primitive ages, we will see that the Third Eye was very much in existence even before the two eyes were formed and became dominant in the later stages. Interestingly, both the two eyes and the pineal gland form out of the tissue layers present in the embryonic brain.

Biology recognizes the pineal gland as nature's first eye, at least in the case of the most primitive vertebrates. Over the centuries, vertebrates and invertebrates have developed eyes of different kinds. This Third Eye is prevalent in the case of fishes, amphibians, and reptiles. One can also find this gland in the birds as well.

Paleontologists claim that dinosaurs had the Third Eye. They are of the opinion that if you see the opening in the skull, you can make out the presence of an eye out there. The later stages of dinosaurs, especially the mammal-like dinosaurs, had these eyes as well, but over the years the eye got receded under the skull and turned into the pineal gland that is found in man and other vertebrates.

There are many who question the existence of God. They are against the belief that God and the human kingdoms gave birth to the plant kingdom and the lower animals rather than the opposite scenario. As per the theospic descriptions, the human being did not come into existence from an end-on transformation of body types. On the contrary, it was the angels who gave birth to the astral models that later on became human beings.

The earliest forms of pre-humans were spiritual beings who had a higher vision and could see the ethereal planes. You may believe in this concept or may not. But don't forget that the earth went through several stages of cooling before it turned into the solid form. So the theospic explanation could be valid.

As per H. P. Blavatsky, in the early stages of the third root race, the physical nature was more of a plastic kind compared to the present day form. More than 18 million years ago, these developments, in culmination with the consciousness factor, led to the formation of the psychological aspect which aimed to perfect the human brain through its association with the physical nature of the brain. This in turn led to the growth of different senses in a more refined way.

As per the Norse mythology, God Odin had to sacrifice one of his eyes so that he could drink from the well of Wisdom. He went ahead and sacrificed the Third Eye. Read through the story of Adam and Eve, and you will find references to the historical evolution of mankind and how with the passage of time, man lost his touch with the Third Eye as he became more and more involved with the daily chores and the materialist things in his life. As he failed to make use of his Third Eye, it became dormant over the years and gradually receded.

Every phase of growth and evolution reflects its set of wisdom and intelligence. It is up to us to activate our Third Eye, and channelize it so that we can surround ourselves with positive energy. If we are looking for inner peace and happiness and want to develop our intuition and sixth sense, then we have no option but to turn to the awakening of the Third Eye.

Even today, the pea shaped pineal gland is the source of our intuition and awareness level. Whenever we have a hunch about something, this gland starts to vibrate gently, which in turn lead to our intuition about the particular incident.

As we begin the journey for spiritual growth and development, we have to monitor and balance our energies so that the awakening of the Third Eye becomes possible. The best and the most effective way to master the art is by practicing unselfish qualities of character and intuition in our daily activities so that, with the passage of time, we can awaken and control our Third Eye.

Chapter 19: Third Eye Chakra Healing

What is Third Eye Chakra Healing

The Third Eye Chakra – also called the Sixth Chakra, and Brow Chakra, and Ajna Chakra – is located between the eyebrows in the center of the brain. The pituitary gland, hypothalamus, and the autonomic nervous system, are governed by the third eye chakra. It is the energy center for our "sixth sense", intuitive perception, psychic abilities, and visualization. The third eye chakra is associated the element Light, the sense of Intuition, and the color Indigo.

Third eye chakra healing is about having control of how to open and close the third eye. Brow chakra healing will open up your psychic abilities – clairvoyance (seeing), clairaudience (hearing), clairsentience (feeling), and claircognizance (knowing/clear thought). Third eye opening is about being able to receive intuitive information, and about having a greater control over your mind and emotions. When your third eye chakra is awakened and balanced you will experience high mental ability, clear thinking, focus, and good health. You will also be able to combine emotion and logic, and separate imagination from reality. Having your third eye opening can also help with fatigue, sleep problems, day dreaming, disorientation, inability to listen to others, empathy of others, and gaining self confidence.

How to Open and Heal the Third Eye Chakra

When your sixth chakra Ajna, has been blocked for a longer period, you will begin to experience emotional and/or physical health problems (see symptoms of a blocked brow chakra below). Third eye chakra healing will open, awaken, and balance your sixth chakra Ajna. You will begin to allow the life force to flow freely again with third eye opening healing sessions.

Opening the third eye chakra will not only cure the symptoms, it will also heal the root problems! As your sixth chakra is balanced, it will positively affect the other chakras as well since they work as one system. This means that the healing benefits from third eye opening will appear in several areas of your life.

There are different third eye opening techniques, and we have gathered some of the most effective and powerful healing techniques that you can apply on yourself to awaken and balance your sixth chakra Ajna:

* Affirmations

* Third Eye Chakra Stones & Crystals

* Essential Oils

* Foods

* Ajna Yoga

* Third Eye Meditation – Ajna Chakra Meditation

* Sound Healing

So, what problems can these third eye opening techniques assist you with? What are the sings of a blocked brow chakra?

How can Third Eye Chakra Healing be of help? Third Eye Opening benefits?

Third chakra healing can help you with headaches, migraines, sleeping problems, fatigue, dizziness, day dreaming, and disorientation. Opening your third eye can also assist in increasing your self confidence. Your listening skills will improve and you will become more empathetic with third eye opening sessions. Improved memory, improved learning ability, and enhanced intuition, are also benefits of awakening the third eye. When you are in the process of opening the third eye chakra you will start experiencing higher states of consciousness and receive guidance from your higher self and Spirits.

Signs of an imbalanced brow chakra or Ajna chakra include: headaches, migraines, dizziness, nausea, learning disabilities, panic, depression, seizures, tumors, brain cysts, problems with eyesight, hearing, balance, and the spinal cord. Make sure to seek medical attention if you are having any of these symptoms. Third eye chakra healing is not a medical treatment, but a complimentary healing method.

Do you need Third Eye Chakra Healing / Third Eye Opening?

You could really benefit from applying some of the third eye opening techniques described below, if you suffer from low self confidence, headaches, migraines, nausea, dizziness, panic attacks, hearing problems, eyesight problems, or depression. Also, if you have learning difficulties, lack common sense, need to improve your listening skills, lack empathy, are judgmental, are over intellectual, or don't listen to your intuition, you probably need third eye chakra healing, as these problems are related to the sixth chakra Ajna.

Do you have a balanced, deficient, or an excessive Third Eye Chakra?

If you experience any of the third eye chakra imbalance symptoms mentioned above, you either have a deficient energy, or an excessive energy in your sixth chakra Ajna. Learn about the general characteristics of a balanced, deficient, and excessive third eye chakra and find out which you have:

A balanced third eye chakra: learn things easily, have great memory, determined, strong will power, intuitive, receive messages from spirit guides, open to a higher consciousness & wisdom, connected to your Divinity and fully understand how to be/do/have anything you want, have out of body experiences / astral travel

A deficient third eye chakra: difficulty in learning things, inability to focus, bad memory, no connection between outer reality and your inner world, no spiritual understanding, no common sense, lacking intuition, have little or no empathy to others An excessive third eye chakra: stressed, suffer from headaches /migraines, judgmental, over-intellectual, overpowering others, unsympathetic, living in a fantasy world, delusional, hallucinating.

If you have a deficient or excessive third eye chakra, it can be a good idea to heal the sixth chakra as the healing process will balance the energy in this center. The following third eye chakra healing techniques & tools will open, awaken, balance and heal the sixth chakra Ajna: affirmations, third eye chakra stones & crystals, essential oils, foods, Ajna yoga, third eye meditation / Ajna chakra meditation, and sound healing.

Learn about the different third eye chakra opening and awakening techniques and choose the ones that you feel guided to. Remember that the healing process should never be "work". Make the healing process of the sixth chakra fresh and fun. Alternate between the different techniques, and enjoy the healing benefits!

Third Eye Opening & Healing – AFFIRMATIONS

Third eye chakra healing affirmations can be helpful in opening, awakening, and balancing the sixth chakra Ajna. You will connect to a higher consciousness as you state these powerful affirmations on a regular basis described below. Work with the ones that resonate with your sixth chakra (brow chakra). Write down the third eye opening & healing affirmations, and place them where you can see them often – on the fridge, on the mirror, on your computer, in your wallet, in your car, in your office, in your locker etc. Make sure to only do your third eye chakra healing affirmations when you feel good, since you affirm with your vibration.

I am wise, intuitive and connected with my inner guide

I am in touch with my inner guidance

I listen to the wisdom within me

146

I trust my intuition to guide and protect me

I understand the "big picture"

I always understand the true meaning of life situations

I know that all is well in my world

I trust that whatever comes to me is for my greatest joy and highest good

I am open to inspiration and bliss

I imagine, I envision, I dream, I know, I see

I am perfectly attuned to my vision

I move toward my vision with purpose and clarity

I am connected to my Divinity

I am at peace

Third Eye Chakra STONES & CRYSTALS

Crystal healing is often applied by energy healers for third eye opening and balancing. The color of the third eye chakra (brow chakra) is indigo; the color of spirituality and wisdom. This is why many third eye chakra stones and crystals have the color indigo/purple.

You can also use third eye chakra stones on yourself, to open and balance your sixth chakra Ajna. Wear these lovely third eye crystals as jewelry, or place them under your pillow as you sleep, and enjoy the healing benefits at the same time! However, another way that is probably more effective for third eye opening is to use them during meditation. Next time you meditate, place the healing stone on your sixth chakra. Visualize how the color indigo is vibrating on your third eye chakra (brow chakra), and imagine how your third eye chakra opens up. Below are examples of powerful third eye chakra stones and crystals that you can use to open and balance your sixth chakra Ajna:

amethyst

azurite

blue aventurine

blue fluorite

blue sapphire

blue tourmaline

kyanite

labrodite

lapiz lazuli

lolite

opal

purple fluorite

sodalite

tanzanite

Third Eye Opening & Healing – ESSENTIAL OILS

Working with essential oils for third eye opening and third eye chakra healing is a lovely way to relax and enjoy the healing benefits at the same time. Your memory, learning ability, intelligence, common sense, and intuition will improve, as your sixth chakra Ajna (third eye chakra / brow chakra) becomes more balanced.

Awakening the third eye chakra doesn't need to be difficult. Just add a few drops into your bath, mix a few drops with your massage oil, or use an oil burner / diffuser. Below are examples of essential oils that can be very powerful for third eye opening and third eye chakra healing:

clary sage

elemi

frankincense

lavender

jasmine

melissa

helichrysum

patchouli

rose

sandalwood

vetiver

Third Eye Opening & Healing – FOODS

There are certain foods that can fuel the third eye chakra (brow chakra). Third eye chakra healing foods are often purple or dark blue in color, and they nourish the brain and mood. Here are examples on what you can eat and drink to awaken your sixth chakra / third eye chakra.

acai berries

blackberries

blueberries

chocolate

cranberries

eggplants

grape juice

lavender spice

mugwort

pomegranate

poppy seed

raspberries

red grapes

red wine

Third Eye Opening & Healing – Ajna YOGA

Yoga is very effective for third eye opening and awakening. The sixth chakra or Ajna Chakra, is both the perception and command center. It is from here you recall past events or last night's dream, and it is also from here you imagine, visualize, and create and your future. There are certain Ajna Yoga poses that can help optimizing your brain functions. These Ajna positions will also open your sixth chakra and allow the life force to flow to the other chakras as well. This means that your overall health will start to improve. As the third eye chakra (brow chakra) is awakened and balanced, your intuition and psychic abilities will develop. You will open up to a higher consciousness and wisdom, and connect to your own Divinity.

The following Ajna Yoga poses are very powerful for third eye opening and awakening. They will balance your sixth chakra Ajna:

The Child Pose – Balasana

The Child pose, or Balasana, is great for third eye awakening as it stimulates the sixth chakra Ajna. Furthermore, this Ajna Yoga pose calms the brain, and relieves stress, fatigue, back pain and neck pain. It also stretches the hips, thighs and ankles.

Standing Half Forward Bend – Ardha Uttanasana

Standing Half Forward Bend, or Ardha Uttanasana, is a great Ajna Yoga pose as it stimulates and puts pressure on the third eye chakra (brow chakra). Besides awakening the sixth chakra, it will also improve posture and strengthen the back. Furthermore, this Ajna Yoga pose will stretch the front torso and stimulate the belly.

The Shoulder Stand Pose – Sarvangasana

The Shoulder Stand, or Sarvangasana, is a fantastic Ajna Yoga pose as it opens the sixth chakra (third eye chakra) and allows the blood to flow directly into the neck and head. This Ajna Yoga pose comes with many health benefits. It stretches the shoulders and neck, tones the buttocks and legs, improves digestion, helps with fatigue and insomnia, stimulates the thyroid and prostate glands, helps relieve the symptoms of menopause. Furthermore, this Ajna Yoga pose can help with infertility, asthma, sinusitis, and mild depression.

Third Eye Meditation – Ajna Chakra MEDITATION

Third eye meditation, or Ajna chakra meditation is very powerful for third eye opening and balancing. You will connect to a higher wisdom and guidance as your sixth chakra Ajna is balanced. As you apply Ajna chakra meditation, try and visualize the color indigo; the color of the third eye chakra (brow chakra). Imagine how an indigo light is vibrating in your sixth chakra Ajna, and how it opens the third eye chakra.

Below are third eye meditation / Ajna chakra meditation videos that you can use to awaken, clear and balance your sixth chakra (brow chakra):

Third Eye Opening & Healing – SOUND HEALING

Sound healing can be very powerful for third eye opening and balancing. As your sixth chakra Ajna is awakened you will connect to your higher consciousness and your psychic powers. The third eye chakra (brow chakra) resonates with a specific color, note, and Hz:

Color Indigo – Note A – 852 Hz

Solfeggio frequencies is a sound healing tool that can be very effective in awakening the third eye chakra. The solfeggio frequency for the third eye chakra (brow chakra) is at 741 Hz. This frequency is about connecting to your spirituality and opening up to a higher consciousness and guidance. Listen to this third eye chakra healing frequency (see videos below) on a regular basis to open and balance your sixth chakra Ajna. It's best to use headphones for optimal healing benefits. Enjoy!

Chapter 20: Awaken Your Inner Self

Meditation is a great way to become more mindful of your thoughts and to get in touch with your inner self. Doing so brings you the clarity of mind to determine what it is you want out of life. In this fast-paced world, we often forget to check in with our true desires in exchange for meeting deadlines and catering to others.

A simple practice of meditation every day can get you back in touch with your mind, opening doors and possibilities all around you. Getting started with meditation is easy. It does not require any fancy equipment or atmosphere. All you need is a quiet space, a willing mind and a little bit of time.

There are many different types of meditation, so finding something that speaks to you will be the goal. There is no right or wrong way to do it, so long as you feel refreshed and renewed with the practice. If you are new to meditation, it may help to have a few guided sessions to get a feel for it.

The idea is very simple, and can easily be done on your own. Find a quiet, comfortable room. Find a comfy chair or sit upright on your bed. Avoid laying down, as you may simply fall asleep. Dim the lights if possible and remove any distractions. Leave your cell phone and computer in another room.

Start breathing in and out, slowly and steadily, focusing on the sound of your breath. Put your energy into listening intently on this sound, and don't let your mind wander to other things. Just be at the moment. If it helps, using a guided meditation soundtrack or chanting can help focus the thought. Sometimes focusing on the breath actually quickens it, which isn't what we want.

This is really it. The goal is to relax your brain, giving it a break from the tireless thoughts of the day. You should feel relaxed and refreshed, ready to think fresh, positive thoughts for the rest of the day. With practice, it will become easier to get yourself to this state.

For more advanced practice, and to focus in on your inner self and your true desires, guided thought meditation can certainly help. Use the meditation time more actively and ask yourself to imagine what it is you want your life to look like. Ask your mind to conjure up a detailed image of what that looks like. Ask for clarity and guidance to reach those goals.

This may not come easily, so don't become frustrated. If it has been a long time since you have listened to your inner self, it may be difficult to get in touch and really know what you want. With practice, those details will begin to emerge. Stay true to your practice every day, and soon you will be able to envision what it is you really need.

With meditation, you can also maneuver through your energy field. Once you get to a good state, begin to imagine that your body is a magnet, and envision the world around you as an infinite energy field. Everything around you gives energy. Look outside to see the trees and grass, the sky and the clouds. It all emits energy, look at it vibrating. Now imagine all of that energy drawing toward you, entering your body through the very crown of your head.

Feel it encircle your entire body. It enters from above but quickly engulfs your belly area, swirling around all of your organs, and soon finding its way to each finger and toe. It courses through you, invigorating every cell. Feel it wash every negative thought from your mind, and replace it with purity and positivity.

Keep in mind that because energy is constantly moving and changing, you cannot expect your meditation to remain constant. Changing your technique and following your inner needs will help ensure that you are getting the most from your practice.

In case you need more reasons besides inner peace to practice meditation, studies show that regular meditation improves mental stability, improves concentration and productivity, enhances relationships and supports good physical health as well. It lowers stress, therefore reducing blood pressure and heart disease. The benefits are outstanding for such a simple practice. Why not get started today? Right now?

Awaken Your Intuition

Our natural intuition is what helps guide our decision making. It is the gut feeling we get when something doesn't feel quite right. The decisions made by intuition don't always make rational sense to the brain, but that is because we are listening to our inner wisdom, which has a broader scope of information to go on. Your intuition is something that has always been with you and continues to try and catch your attention, but you are not listening.

You may be out of touch with your intuition if you are feeling generally unguided. You may feel as if even small decisions are difficult to make, and those decisions may lead you down a path that does not suit your best interests. If this sounds like the course of your life right now, it is time to get back on track by tapping into your natural intuition.

Being more mindful of your thoughts and subtle feelings throughout the day is a great way to get in touch with your intuition. We often ignore feelings of discomfort or dissatisfaction for the perceived greater good. We continue to go to jobs we don't really like for the sake of affording the bills. We continue to see specific friends even though they don't bring out our best selves. It is often easier to carry out these comfortable tasks to make things easier, as change can be difficult.

Now is the time to embrace the idea of bigger and better things. Are you truly happy with your job? Your circle of friends? Do you like the way you feel waking up in the morning, or do you feel unhealthy? Being honest with yourself will help make those tough decisions much easier. Stop burying those intuitive feelings and let them bubble to the surface.

If you aren't sure exactly how to simply 'listen' to yourself, try doing more creative things to get the juices flowing. This could be anything from keeping a journal of your thoughts and feelings, to various types of art. It could be gardening and connecting more deeply with nature, or simply being more attentive to your thoughts.

Being creative is an activity of the spirit. When we do things like balancing the checkbook or do household chores, there is already a basic template for how it should be done. The framework for these tasks is always the same and doesn't allow any opportunity for the brain to stretch beyond its current capacity. However, creating something out of nothing is an exercise, something that requires inner strength, confidence, and guidance.

If you have ever written a book or created a piece of art, you may understand this feeling. Beyond the physical act of typing away at your keyboard or applying paint to a canvas, you actually go into a sort-of trance as you work. Your analytical brain takes a break, and your creative brain goes on autopilot. The result is a piece of work that has come directly from your inner spirit, something your analytical brain could have never imagined.

Once you find something creative that you love, let your spirit take off. Do whatever it is your spirit compels you to do. Experiment with new types of paints, try clay, take a hike in a new area, whatever the case may be. Learning to follow this intuition in a controlled environment actually trains you to let intuition take over when it really counts. As you practice these skills, you will realize that they have the same application in everyday life.

Your job can be run the same way. Allow some creativity to hold your interest, and if your intuition is leaving you blank, maybe it is time to make a shift in your life. Asking for new assignments that compel your creativity and intuition become your new art, and success is sure to follow. Remaining stagnant and following the same pattern does not allow that intuition to grow and change, which it will naturally want to do.

No matter how you choose to listen, harness the power of your intuition and don't be afraid to follow it. The biggest mistake you can make is hearing your intuition and squashing its power by not making any necessary changes. Life is all about flow and change. Staying stagnant and refusing to make important decisions do not keep us in good pace with the energy of the universe. Learning to fully function with intuition as our guide will ensure we are abreast of all of the positive things that may come our way.

Chapter 21: Tips On How To Activate Your Third Eye

Now connecting to your third eye is like open up a connection to all the answers that the universe is waiting to give to you. So, what are some of the things that you can do to open your third eye?

Listen to Binaural Beats Music

The first one is to listen to binaural beats music. Now alpha waves and binaural beat music will help to raise your frequency. However, you need to use a headset to listen to them because they play different sounds within the ear.

Use herbal teas

The second one is to use herbal teas. Herbs are a very important drink that will help to align your third eye. You can order take a cup of tea that has bright blueberries, lavender, or rosemary or you could also buy a third eye Buddha tea to help open your third eye that is if you don't want to go to a grocery store and spend a hundred bucks to buy lavender and all the different fancy ingredients. If you want something fast and easy, then get the Buddha tea. And as you drink the tea, try to make it a whole ritual instead of just drinking the tea like a magic potion. Now when drinking the tea, you can just sit down quietly and enjoy the whole process and visualize that your third eye is opening up as you are drinking the tea.

Meditate with crystals

The next step is to meditate with crystals. Now when trying to open up your third eye and try to meditate and bring stillness to your mind, so that you'll be able to hear your third eye and your intuition and your psychic self. You need to be able to make space for that. You can make a crown or headband that you can wear while meditating so that one of the Crystals will go over your third eye and then you will use the side ones to go over the sides of your heads, and another one will go over the back of your head. You can crystal use it when you are meditating or when you're are trying to do something creative like drawing or writing because it can help to give you that psychic boost.

So, if you are lying down, you can place it at the hemisphere crystal or the lapis crystal and then lay down and chant on for about 108 times. Now when you do the chant "om," try to feel the vibration on your third eye, which is the vibration that stimulates your pineal gland and activates your third eye. Also, don't forget to clean and charge your crystals before using them so you can smoke them or wash them in saltwater under the moonlight.

Practice Yoga

Another way to activate your third eye is to practice yoga. Yoga positions like the down dog position, the mounting pose, the child pose is all great pose for activating your today.

Eat Alkaline Foods

The next step is to eat alkaline foods. Start eating and drinking foods that are alkaline in nature; these include grains, pawpaw, vegetables, beans, seeds, and nuts. All these foods help to detox your pineal gland. They help to calcify your pineal gland. Alkaline-forming foods also help to detox your pineal gland and cleanse your body while balancing the pH levels of your body. They also increase the level of your intuition and overall well-being. They also help to prevent further calcification.

Avoid Flouride

The next tips are to avoid fluoride. Avoid anything that has fluoride whenever you can. Fluoride is mostly contained in toothpaste and water. So, try to use toothpaste that is fluoride-free because fluoride calcifies the pineal gland and makes it more difficult for you to use your third eye.

Use Essential Oils

The next step is to use essential oils like sanding wood or frankincense and put certain drops of those oil on your finger and do the circular motion a few times with your hands and then sit there quietly and visualize your third eye just opening up.

Take Salt Balts

The next step is to Bath with sea salt. Take a bath with indigo color sea salt. Put the salt into the water and then enter the bathtub with the intention that once you get into the bathtub, you will like to clear and open up your third eye.

When you slow down and meditate using all these things to activate your third eye, what you are really trying to do is creating space in between your thinking so that you can hear the message that is meant to guide you on your part. So always remember to listen to binaural beat music, drink, herbal teas meditate with crystals.

Chapter 22: Build Connection With Inner Psychic Abilities

To help prevent from having the negative symptoms of Third Eye Awakening such as feeling confused, or disoriented, you need to build a connection with the energy of the elements and nature so that you can develop your psychic abilities. Try to open up gradually and explore your extrasensory perceptions. If you learn to activate the theta and alpha brainwaves, it will make the brain more receptive and develop your frontal lobe activity. You can start this by meditating on the Third Eye such as visualizing on the subtle indigo, blue or purple colors that help trigger the sixth chakra. You can add these colors to your home décor, clothing, wear jewelries, consume food with natural purple/ blue hues and let the energy flow. To keep it under control, do conscious breathing so that it allows cleansing your inner self. Try to perceive things with much clarity as possible so that the energy running through you can appear through your

What is unseen in the eyes of the normal minds are revealed into the subtle dimensions of the Third Eye, even though these unfamiliar and unusual perceptions may seem disturbing to the ordinary mind.

Since the birth, we had the Third Eye as part of our energetic body which cultivated the willpower, truth, trust, and confidence. With the Third Eye Awakening, they can be re-activated in a way that catches the vibes of the spiritual domain. So, to change your life in a positive way, your body requires the Third Eye Awakening so that you can put the negative energy and troubled experiences behind to experience new life. So begin your spiritual practice and put your faith on it, so that can unlock your intuition and sense of understanding the life's path. Your personal experiences and insights of the happenings around you will elevate your spiritual perceptions.

Chapter 23: Achieving Higher Consciousness

Mankind has always tried to find ways to fight stress, anxieties, and worries in spirituality and devotion. When questions become too confusing and your mind has no answers, you turn to the powers of the unseen. Science couldn't understand it and hence rejected it. The same was the fate of the concept of the third eye. Our ancestors across all cultures of the east and the west have believed in the concept of the third eye. They believed that it had the answers to the most complex problems. Modern medicine leaves many people to understand that they should only consider what can be seen, heard, or touched. Stress, anxiety, and worry remained problems that could only be treated through pills. Such treatments only treat symptoms and are never lasting.

Until recently, the third eye was considered a concept suited for the occult or an idea favored by spirituality. Scientists were not ready to believe that such amazing things could be done with simple techniques like meditation. They thought the higher sense of perception or consciousness was not possible in general. This has been answered now. New research carried out by neurologists and psychotherapists have changed the way science looks at the pineal gland now.

Serotonin and melatonin are two important hormones stimulated by the pineal. It is known now that these hormones play a very important role in regulating your mood and cycles of sleep and wakefulness. These two things have a profound impact on the way we function in life. Our knowledge and experience of the world as we know it is governed by these things. In a mental state of unpleasantness, you will not be able to enjoy even the most beautiful things in the world. If you are sad, stressed, or unhappy, even the tastiest food would not look appealing to you. In opposition, when you feel pleasant, even your least favorite foods might taste slightly better to you. The pineal gland regulates both these hormones. If your pineal gland is functioning smoothly, you can keep stress and anxiety at bay.

Meditation has been considered as one of the most effective ways to activate the pineal gland and improve its abilities. Science has proven that meditation can bring real physiological changes in the brain that help in the evolution and growth of the pineal gland. This makes the concept of higher consciousness a possibility.

Meditation also helps in reducing the release of the stress hormone called cortisol. This hormone can start several negative processes. It has a strong physiological impact on your body. From obesity to adverse inflammatory responses, cortisol is a big offender. Meditation can help you in suppressing the release of this hormone.

It has also been proven that an active pineal gland can help you in bringing down your sense of fear. If your sense of fear goes down, you won't show frequent 'fight or flight' responses at the drop of a hat. Your reactions to situations will become subtler.

Sages, seers, monks, and people indulged in devotion are known to show reduced signs of fear. Spiritual consciousness brings down such responses. We now know that spirituality has a deep connection with the pineal gland and the third eye. The third eye opens the gate for spiritual consciousness. Your sixth chakra helps you in raising your consciousness and opening up the seventh chakra of the spiritual dimension.

So, if your pineal gland is healthy and your third eye is active, you will have fewer worries. Your anxiety levels would go down. Your reactions to situations in life become stable, and you react in a calm and composed manner.

Our reactions to situations are as per our worldly experience and the way our brain processes that information. Between your eye and the pineal gland lies the very important orbitofrontal cortex. It gathers information as you view and experience things in the outside world and distributes it to the other parts of the brain for use. This is the primary point where all information comes and goes. The output of this part would dictate your behavior, emotional, and physiological responses.

A healthy pineal gland working with the orbitofrontal cortex helps in forming a sync between the information that's coming and going. An increased sense of consciousness led by the pineal gland can help in bringing stable reactions. Your level of tolerance to situations can rise phenomenally. The pineal gland can help in moderating reactions to a great extent. People who meditate for longer periods and have a healthy pineal and an activated third eye will have very controlled heart rate, blood flow, pain threshold, etc.

The hippocampus in our brain is one specific area that has a deep impact on your memory and consciousness. You can proactively work to expand your hippocampus through third eye meditation. It is humanly possible to do this knowingly. Stress, on the other hand, can lead to shrinkage in the size of the hippocampus. The more stressful you remain, the lower would be your levels of consciousness.

Therefore, it is possible to get over the feelings of stress, anxiety, and worry. These are responses to the way our brain processes the information received from the world. We can actively improve the mechanism that processes this information correctly.

Stress, worry, and anxiety kick in the survival mechanism. These feelings keep us confined to the roots. We always remain busy with thoughts of self-preservation and never look beyond although we want to do so.

A quest for knowledge and a sense of greater purpose has always intrigued humankind. Survival hasn't been the sole focus of our race, and this makes us different from other species. The third eye helps us in this pursuit.

We have always aspired to look beyond the limits of the things that can be seen. We want to know things that are beyond comprehension. We all want to know what is in store for us in the future. However, all this isn't possible through the available physical means. The physical eyes have limitations. This is the point from which the all-seeing third eye gains prominence.

The third eye can help us in having a greater vision. It brings with itself the power of wisdom and foresight. It opens the portals to cosmic vision. It is believed that the awakened third eye can dilute the barriers of time and space. It works beyond the known four dimensions.

The physical location of the mystical third eye is the pineal gland. Once activated, this gland can help you in gaining greater consciousness and also psychic abilities. The ethereal energy in your body becomes intense.

Activating the third eye will help you in rising above these restrictions. It will expand the depth of your thought and consciousness. You will experience the world in a new light.

Chapter 24: Technique of Clearing Your Mind

There is a tiny bit of vibration present in you at your Third Eye forehead area. This technique is meant to reveal this vibration to you so that you can cultivate it. And this technique is meant to be practiced once to awaken your Third Eye. After that, you should continue with other meditation techniques.

First, choose a good day to do this. Choose a low-stress day with low to little foreseeable stress ahead of you. It is best to start this on a day right before a full moon if at all possible. As always, choose a good location. You should find a quiet place with little disturbances or distractions. You can do this alone, or with a friend, or in a group. The experience can be far more intense with a like-minded group.

Before you start, you should understand that this is not a meditation technique at all. It is not visualization. It's a technique where you clear your mind of absolutely everything. The idea is to fully relax, to fully clear your mind, and fully open your spirit up to being filled. There should be no imagining, no visualization, and no thinking. You should let the experience come to you.

For this one, lie down flat on the floor. Place your hands next to your side, extending down the side of your body, with your palms up. Your legs should be straight, with your eyes closed.

Relax. Use a breathing technique. Focus on your breathing for several minutes.

Now you should start a throat vibration. (You can practice this beforehand.) Let your breath roll over your voice box and cause a vibration. This should be low and subtle. It's not about the noise. It's about the vibration. As the air flows over your voice box, you will feel a vibration from the friction, and hear a low humming. Don't worry whether it is exactly right. Keep it up for several minutes (for up to about ten minutes).

Your goal here is to "be aware" without thinking or imaging. Just be aware. Let your mind float. Let it be free. Let any energy you feel flow through you. If you feel a movement or tingle in your body, don't stop it or think about it. Just let it happen.

After about ten minutes of this, raise one of your hands over your face. With your palm facing your face, put the center of your palm right over your forehead area, and at a point between your eyes. Do not touch any part of your face. Hold your hand very close to your face without touching it. Stay in this position. Keep breathing. Keep your eyes closed. Keep your throat vibrating. Be aware of your Third Eye forehead area.

After about ten minutes, lower your hand back to the floor. Keep up your throat vibrations.

You should become aware of a vibration between your eyes or within your forehead. You might feel this as a tingling or a buzzing or a vibration. It could feel like a pressure or weight just within your head.

Keep your mind clear. Let it happen. Keep your eyes closed.

When you become aware of your forehead vibration, connect it with your throat vibrations mentally. Be aware of both vibrations and feel them merge as one.

If you feel sensations in other parts of your body, ignore them. Let them happen. That is normal for this process.

Let this process continue for about ten minutes, having no thoughts, no visualizations, and no meditations. Keep a clear mind. Relax and experience the ride.

Now stop the throat vibrations. Lay calm and keep still. Keep your eyes closed. Do not try to be aware of anything, even the vibrations. Be only aware of the Third Eye area of your forehead. Do this for about another ten minutes.

If you feel or experience light or colors or energy between your eyes or within your forehead or head, this is your Third Eye activating.

Chapter 25: For the Clients

Why then are some readings accurate and some not?

Again because some psychics aren't that good at what they do. Or the person being read has a block against being read. Or since all experience is comprised of thought, a client, being forewarned, can decide not to allow a prediction to happen if he doesn't want that result. But if you believe you are not in control of your fate, that what the psychic says HAS to happen, then it will.

Another very strong reason is that the client may not have any focused thoughts or plans in his or her mind. In that case, there is nothing to read for the future. Your future depends greatly on your goals. Some people just float along, never deciding or determining what they want to do in their lives. You actually have to want something if you are going to get something. As in the old Rogers and

Hammerstein song, "You got to have a dream if you want to have a dream come true."

Psychics read what is going on in your mind. You really do need to be focused on something to happen if you want a reading to be accurate.

Because the psychic is usually reading your own mind or aura, the information is taken from you yourself. You may have decided that something is going to happen in your life; or you are afraid something is going to happen or, alternately, hoping that something is going to happen. The psychic reads your thoughts and speaks them aloud and you can accept them or prevent them form happening. If much of this book seems repetitive, it is on purpose. It's very important to understand the power of your own mind and how subtle suggestions can make you cause events subconsciously.

Some predictions are given on the basis of warning someone that something will happen if they follow a certain path. For example, being told not to get on a plane, and you heed the warning, and the plane crashes. Being told to get to a doctor because your body is developing a problem that is not yet strong enough to be felt.

This takes us to another area of interest. Sometimes a psychic will pick up an illness and mention it, and it is something that already has happened, or it has happened to someone close to the client. Again, a person carries many issues and thoughts with him. Sometimes if someone's spouse or child has experienced a traumatic event, you will "read" it on the client. Here is where you should not just blindly go into a person's aura and start assuming that everything in his consciousness pertains to him or her. Knowing what you are receiving and why is a major tool in focusing more precisely on your client.

I have some examples that illustrate this point. One friend of mine, who was into evangelistic Christianity, went to a demonstration by another Christian who called himself a "prophet." What he did was psychic readings for the people there. My friend received a reading that had nothing to do with him. The "prophet" told him he was interested in wood-working and used power tools and built many things through carpentry. My friend did not verify the reading to the "prophet."

He came to see me and told me what the man had read for him and said he was confused because it was all wrong, and supposedly it came from God. I recognized immediately that the man had done a reading that applied directly to my roommate who had a shed full of power tools and was always building things from furniture to add on rooms. I told him and he saw that was right.

"But how could that happen?" he asked. He had in his mind that the reader, who identified himself with God as a prophet, could not be wrong if he was receiving the message direct from God. It took some time to navigate through that, explaining that just because someone decides he is a God-inspired prophet doesn't mean he is, and it is easy to pick up something in your mind about someone else, if the images are strong. Basically he was having his mind read, but an area that was not about him.

Psychics need not to set themselves up as infallible, especially when dealing with such an area. And they should not assume that they are like the Prophets in the Bible because they can read that someone works with carpentry. Before doing nay kind of work as a professional you should have your act together as a professional, and at least have a rudimentary education in how your talent works...or if it works at all.

In New York many years ago I went to a psychic who a friend asked me to visit because she was consulting with him and was confused by his readings. I went and the psychic told me that there was going to be a horrible murder at my house, with someone being stabbed to death and involving a lot of blood. Uplifting as it was, I had my doubts as it didn't ring true to me.

The next day the psychic called me almost ecstatic.

"Did you see the paper today?" he asked.

"I said, which one?'

He told me that it was on the front page of the Daily News and was very excited. Someone had been stabbed to death in front of his own building a few hours after I'd left. I told him that was horrible, why was he so happy?

"Don't you remember? I predicted it would happen?"

I reminded him that he was doing a reading for me, and if he'd got it right he might have been able to stop the murder before it happened. I dismissed him in my mind. He called me again a few weeks later and asked if I wanted another reading! Firs of all, that was so unprofessional I couldn't believe he called.

I reminded him that all of what he told me was about other people (as it turned out). He said, well, you can't always know what it's about.

I told him that therefore the readings were worthless and I wasn't going to pay him to just read the ethers, so to speak. So you see this area gets kind of iffy when people doing it won't take pains to hone their ability.

Sometimes a psychic must also discriminate about what the client wants to know. You should not act as a paid spy for example, if they want to know what an ex-husband is doing and with whom. I remember one reading where a woman wanted to know if her ex-husband was out womanizing in bars. I saw him in a bar, but also saw that he was wishing she were with him, not picking up other women as she thought. I just told her that she might want to re-establish communication with him to be sure she wasn't making a mistake in the divorce. It was none of her business what her ex-husband was doing. She was still obsessed about him.

Some clients really are not parasites, even when they ask for many readings on a regular basis. I had one young male client, who was confused about his feelings for a woman and was unable to decide to actually marry her. He had other issues from his childhood that needed to be resolved that were preventing him from making a commitment of marriage much as he wanted it. Because all our readings had been on the phone, and I had never met him, I had been able to keep myself neutral in his life and he was able to ask about things he had not been able to address with a therapist or with his father, where the conflict originated. I was able to maintain a continuing series of consultations with him because he had no interest in pulling me into his life, I was more or less a "talking head." He wanted someone anonymous who was speaking from an objective point as he saw it.

At a certain point he felt confident enough to open more to his therapist and his father and fiancée, and my readings were no longer required. I was invisible, yet could answer his questions, and he built up enough security to talk about it a second time to people who really could help him break through. He did it all himself.

There was a side dish to this, which was somewhat amusing. The girlfriend had somehow learned he was calling me and she called pretending to be asking about a "friend of hers whose boyfriend couldn't decide to marry her." One should understand that psychic ability often means you can't pull that kind of lie on a psychic. Later, she admitted to him that she'd done it and he told me, but I already knew. One can always indulge young lovers.

There are times when the truth hurts. In one case I did readings for a man who was in love with a beautiful young woman. He asked if it would work out. I ran the cards several times to make sure of what they were getting. Each time it was the same: the relationship, quiet and lovely as it was, would not survive. Basically the woman was fond of him and just assumed she would marry him, but in reality wasn't in love with him. When she would meet someone she did love it would be disaster. If it ended before marriage his heart would be healable.

Within the same time, without my knowing who she was, she came for a reading and I saw that same thing. She nodded and said she really knew she didn't love him in that way. In fact she had come to have a reading to get a viewpoint that would help her define her hesitation. He was quite upset about it, and later on when I ran into him he glared at me as if I had caused the feeling.

People should not ask for answers if they don't want them.

Another young woman had been sent to me for a reading by her parents, who paid for it. I knew nothing about her situation but saw that she was living with a man who was a drug addict and she was convinced she could help him. The reading showed that he was using her as an enabler instead. I told her and thought no more about it. Later, about a month I ran into her in a store and she was hostile towards me. Then after that her mother came to me and I asked why the daughter seemed angry. She explained that they thought she had been set up, that she thought they had briefed me about her situation and wanted me to pretend I was getting it psychically as a way to get her to leave him. It was odd. She didn't really believe in psychic ability and wouldn't accept that I had read the situation as it stood.

This is how negative energy can come to you without your even knowing.

Fortunately I always protect myself before and after readings, but if I had been upset or cared about their reactions they could have invaded me negatively. It is important for a psychic to completely flush out the reading after the client leaves. This is a very real thing to deal with and you should not treat it lightly.

It's mainly due to this factor that I try not do readings for money. These readings I did do for money. There is no morality about it, but there is a real need to be able to pick and choose whom you read for.

There are times that a psychic gets greedy. It doesn't come under the heading of evil but it does sound sleazy when it happens, and discredits the person who is psychic. One example happened to me many years ago. I was getting a reading on the phone by a man who had been referred by a friend. During the reading he started out by giving me some lottery numbers. In a rapid sequence he told me the numbers and without pausing said, "...and, George, I want my share." It happened fast and I stopped and thought, "does he want me to share the winnings if I play?"

That is exactly what he meant. As it happened I never bothered playing the numbers, but decided to check them out. I would have had to play them for about ten days before they would come up, although he was right, they did come up as daily winners several times. He must have had some money strains because about a year later I called for a reading and he said his new policy was that you had to send the money first to his son, in another state, then when the check cleared you would get a reading. I figured since I'd had several readings already he might know— without psychic ability -- that I was good for the money, so I never bothered to follow through.

The point is that I am not trying to promote all psychics as either honest, high-minded or even necessarily very intelligent. Many people assume that because a person can do this accurately that he also has some kind of "in" with the

Lord and is a special, almost holy person. People I have read accurately for have treated me with that respect and it was hard to push them towards understanding this was not something better than what they did. That would be wrong to claim. The variations of goodness or evil have nothing to do with psychic ability.

I am also not trying to promote this aspect of the psychic sense as something that is the total sum of what you can do with your mind. Psychic readings are basically one part of how this ability can be used, but it would be limiting to think that's all it is. This sense is at the hart of all you do, all you achieve or don't achieve, what you believe in or doubt – especially yourself.

To close this chapter I would like to address the idea that many psychics have that they cannot read for themselves. Some feel it is a betrayal of their gift. Others find that as a reality, they are never accurate about themselves, mostly because their own fears and emotions enter in and block the information. I always read for myself and have no problem with accuracy. In fact I think if one has a true insight into where the information really comes from, if one removes the veils of mystery so to speak, you can see plainly that you are the best one to read for yourself. It is all just a matter of knowing what is in your own mind. You would not go to a friend and ask them to read a book for you unless you were blind. You listen to your own music, eat your own food and comb your own hair.

As to calling oneself "psychic" it has to be stated that when it comes to using your mind and your talents to achieve or fail, you are as psychic as anyone else. It is not always about reading fortunes or telling the future. It is about knowing who you are and exercising your right to achieve what you want to do. It is about relating to people in ways you want to interact by tuning into them and finding ways to get along.

Using your own pineal gland to find out what you are planning to do at your own subconscious level is the key. It is the same as deciding what art you want to look at and enjoy, what music to listen to with your ears. If you insist that it comes from some place that requires some other entity to "reveal" your own thoughts to you, then you are free to do that. But true happiness comes from being free, and knowing that you make your own destiny.

If a psychic reading enhances that and helps you more easily to assert yourself and control your own mind, then that is a positive use of the talent. Always remember that even if you always consult with a psychic, not to regard the person as a need or a crutch. He is not telling you anything you don't already know.

CPSIA information can be obtained
at www.ICGtesting.com
Printed in the USA
BVHW091358290621
610728BV00003B/916